# Good Mourning

# Good Mourning

### Help and Understanding in Time of Pregnancy Loss

Judy Gordon Morrow &
Nancy Gordon DeHamer

FOREWORD BY DALE HANSON BOURKE

WORD PUBLISHING

Dallas · London · Sydney · Singapore

GOOD MOURNING: HELP AND UNDERSTANDING IN TIME OF PREGNANCY LOSS

Scripture quotations used in this book are from the following sources:

The King James Version of the Bible (KJV).

The New American Standard Bible (NASB), © The Lockman Foundation 1960, 1962, 1963, 1968, 1971, 1972, 1973, 1975, 1977.

The Holy Bible, New International Version (NIV). Copyright © 1973, 1978, 1984 International Bible Society. Used by permission of Zondervan Bible Publishers

The names and certain identifying details have been changed in some of the stories used in this book to preserve the privacy of the parties involved.

**Library of Congress Cataloging-in-Publication Data**

Morrow, Judy Gordon.
    Good mourning : help and understanding in time of pregnancy loss / Judy Gordon Morrow and Nancy Gordon DeHamer.
       p.       cm.
    Bibliography: p.
    ISBN 0-8499-3168-1
    1. Children—Death—Religious aspects—Christianity.
2. Bereavement—Religious aspects—Christianity.  3. Miscarriage.
4. Fetal death.    I.  DeHamer, Nancy Gordon.    II.  Title.
BV4907.M63    1989
248.8'6—dc20                        89-33599
                                            CIP

*Printed in the United States of America*

9 8 0 1 2 3 9 RRD 9 8 7 6 5 4 3 2 1

For my husband, Patrick,
with love and appreciation.
JGM

For David, Diane, Cordy, and Tom,
because you believed in me
and wouldn't let me give up on my dream.
NGD

To have known life within
Is to have known joy
And the freshness of beginnings.
To have that life snatched away
Leaves me with my hands outstretched,
My arms open wide
Feeling emptiness and space,
Rather than the weight of my child
With newborn warmth and silken hair.
My body
So full of kicks and squirms one day,
Is barren and lifeless the next,
Stripped of its child
That I never knew.
Yet I did know
And loved.

Judy Gordon Morrow

# CONTENTS

# ACKNOWLEDGMENTS

We would like to thank the many people whose support was so vital during the writing of this book:

Thank you to . . .

Eileen who, when she was unable to find an appropriate book to give to Judy after the baby's death, was the first to suggest that Judy write her story.

The many women who shared their stories of loss so that other women could find healing. Our special thanks to Marian McDonald, Donna Moriarty, and Mary Davis for permission to quote from previously published works about their losses.

The forty families to whom Judy wrote requesting their prayers as we struggled to complete the writing of this book. What a difference you made!

Judy's caring "work family" at Miguelito school who continually encouraged her through the ups and downs of her writing life.

Judy's writer's group led by Anne, for their untiring listening and helpful suggestions, but most of all for their love and prayers.

Our families who picked up the slack and were a continual source of encouragement to us even when it meant we were not always available to them.

Judy's church family, Trinity Church of the Nazarene, Lompoc, California, whose prayers and support and hugs sustained her from beginning to end.

Nancy's church family, Trinity Covenant Church, Salem, Oregon, for constant encouragement. Special thanks to the Spiritual Encourager's Class of 1986–87 whose prayers and support made all the difference, and whose end-of-the-book pizza party provided motivation to finish the task.

Ann Kiemel Anderson and Dale Hanson Bourke for their enthusiastic support of this book.

All the people at Word Books who have been involved in bringing this book to publication, and especially Beverly Phillips for her guidance and sensitive editing.

# FOREWORD

I remember the day so clearly. It was one of those perfect, warm summer days when you roll down your windows and play your radio and smile at all of the people you pass. Everything about life seemed wonderful.

True, I could hardly get into the car because of my enormous stomach. But I was nearing the end of what my doctor described as "the most trouble-free twin pregnancy" he had ever seen. I was grateful for my health. And I was ready to hold those two little babies I had watched so often on the ultrasound screen.

But I wasn't ready for the news I received in the next hour. Something had happened to one of my babies. The doctor couldn't explain why or how, but my baby girl had died. Tests showed that my other baby was fine—for now. But no one could assure me that he would be all right.

What followed were days of tests and consultations and medical opinions. There were the telephone calls to tell family and friends, questions to be asked and answered, and tears to be cried with my husband, our little boy, friends, and even strangers.

Finally I gave birth to a healthy baby boy and perfectly formed baby girl who had died for reasons we will never know. We were very, very grateful to have one baby to hold and love and take home. But we would never be the same because of our loss.

In the early days of our grieving, many loving friends offered support and comfort. But the greatest help came from one dear woman who had also lost a baby. She knew how I felt. She let me cry and be angry and ask questions. She was not embarrassed by my grief, nor did she try to minimize it. Without her support I don't know how I would have made it.

There were so many times when I asked, "Why isn't there a book to read about this?" I wanted answers to questions, and I wanted to know that I wasn't abnormal in my feelings. I found some resources, but nothing that really spoke to me with understanding, information, and faith.

Nearly a year after losing our baby I came upon the typed manuscript for this book. I read it in one sitting, finally feeling that someone understood what I had been going through. *If only someone had given me this book when I first learned about our baby's death,* I thought. I was moved by the openness of the authors, encouraged by their insights, and helped by their practical approach. My own healing was greatly enhanced by their writing.

If you have lost a baby, whether recently or in the past, I highly recommend this book to you. It will not give you pat answers or underestimate your sorrow. But it will help you understand and grieve in a healthy way and eventually heal.

If you have a friend who is dealing with the loss of a baby, give her this book instead of flowers. It will let her know you care, and it will give her the help she will need in the days ahead.

Most importantly, if you are a pastor, or a doctor, or a counselor, have this book ready to offer to the woman in need. It is balanced and thoughtful and sound. And it is written by someone who deeply understands the pain a woman feels when she says good-bye to a child she will never know.

DALE HANSON BOURKE
Senior Editor,
*Today's Christian Woman*

# INTRODUCTION

*Judy*

I was devastated when our baby died immediately after birth in the fall of 1979. If you, too, have suffered similar loss, my heart goes out to you. How I wish I could look in your eyes and talk with you face to face. I wish I could hug you and cry with you. And then I would listen—listen to your story of heartache and sorrow which is yours alone. Unique. Heartrending. I ache with fresh grief each time I hear of a miscarriage, stillbirth, or loss of a newborn. I will never forget the pain and emptiness.

When our baby died I felt as if I were drowning in my sorrow, and I struggled to even stay afloat. I didn't know my grief and feelings were normal. I didn't know I was entitled to grieve. I didn't know what to do with those feelings that seemed so abnormal to me. I had no idea there was a right way and a wrong way to handle grief. I only knew I hurt and that I wanted it to go away. At that time nothing was written to give me guidance toward healthy grieving, and I floundered in my own misconceptions.

My sister, Nancy, watched me in my struggle, only catching glimpses of it now and then, as many miles separated us. She hurt for me. Eventually we talked . . . and then shared some more. New realizations and healing touched me through her.

The seed for this book was planted years ago by a friend's suggestion that I write my story. Nancy, along with others, encouraged me, sending me articles attached with notes stressing the need for this kind of book. I cried the Christmas I opened Nancy's gift to me—a writing kit to take to the library or a quiet place wherever, complete with a notebook, oodles of supplies, and snacks! Her belief in me and the necessity of sharing my story touched me deeply.

And then in a beautiful chain of events Nancy joined me in the telling of my story, adding to it a new dimension with her reflections and exercises in journal keeping. It has not been an easy task. Nancy lives in Oregon, while I live in California. Many of the women who wrote their stories for us to include also live in other states. Trying to juggle work and home schedules to sandwich in writing time has been challenging at the very least. Yet for every discouragement there were encouragers who said, "Yes, this is needed, don't give up." Others who said, "I have a friend who really needs to hear what you have to say."

In speaking to different women's groups, I have been overwhelmed at the number of women who have experienced pregnancy loss. What has amazed and saddened me even more, however, are the many women who have never worked through the grief and pain of their loss. Some have buried their hurt for decades. Whether your sorrow is hours fresh or covered by many years, it needs to be dealt with in a healthy way. Good mourning is not only possible, it is so necessary for the living out of the rest of our lives.

*Nancy*

For most of our adult life, Judy and I have been separated by many hundreds or thousands of miles. When she lost her baby in 1979, she lived in California; I lived in Iowa. But we talked often by phone, wrote letters, and saw each other occasionally. We talked about her experience of loss and its impact on her life. When she began to think about writing a book about it, I encouraged her to do it.

While she was still going through the first year or two of her grief, I was becoming aware of some needs in my own life. After the birth of my second daughter, almost nine years after the first, I was feeling overwhelmed and isolated from the world around me. Something was not right in my life.

About that time I was invited to join a group of women from my church who met together twice a month to discuss a book they were reading together. When I joined them they were reading *Letters to Scattered Pilgrims* by Elizabeth O'Connor. Early in the book there were two chapters on keeping a journal, and one woman in the group said, "We can't just read this. We need to start keeping a journal ourselves and see if it's as helpful as she says it is."

So I bought a spiral notebook and began to write about my life. I was working full time, my husband was a resident in family practice with a crazy schedule, and my two daughters were nine years old and five months old. Yet somehow I found the time two or three times a week to begin to look at myself, my human relationships, and my relationship with God, and to write about these things in my journal.

The group finished that book and went on to another, but I kept writing in my journal. For it had become a safe place for me—a place to unload some of the feelings I didn't like and didn't understand. It became a place for me to step back and look at how I was reacting in certain situations. As I continued writing, I began to see patterns in my life; not only that, but I also began to see ways I could change those patterns.

For the last nine years my journal has been my companion. When Judy sent me the beginnings of her story a few years ago and said, "What can I do with this to make it more than just another sad story?" I thought of my journal and what it has meant to me as I've lived through the joys and sorrows of my life.

This book is in a sense the intersection of our lives. We are very different sorts of people. Judy is very outgoing, very people oriented. She feels deeply. I'm quieter, more reserved, and tend to be more thought oriented. Together we've tried to write the kind of book that Judy wishes she had had when she was thrust into the world of grief.

When we first began working on this together and I began writing the "Reflection" parts of the book, I felt almost presumptuous in daring to write about pregnancy loss when I'd not had that experience. While we were writing this book, my husband decided to end our seventeen-year marriage. That was a pain I didn't think I would ever have to face. I found myself experiencing many of the same feelings that Judy and the other women who share their stories in this book experienced at the time of their loss. I found writing in my journal through this crisis to be helpful and healing. As a result, I am more convinced than ever of the validity of our approach to the process of grieving loss.

*   *   *   *

Each chapter of *Good Mourning* begins with a part of Judy's story. Following is a section called "Reflections," where the emotional consequences of that aspect of the loss are discussed. This section also includes the stories of several other women who lost a child (or children) during some stage of pregnancy or shortly after birth. Most of these women are personal friends of one or both of us. You will meet many of these women more than once, as their stories are interspersed throughout the book. They willingly shared their painful experiences in the hope that others would be helped. Each chapter concludes with questions for you to write about in a journal, as a way of working through your grief and recording your story.

We offer you this book with a prayer that it will help you on your journey toward wholeness and healing.

JUDY GORDON MORROW
NANCY GORDON DeHAMER

# KEEPING YOUR JOURNAL

Set up road signs;
  put up guideposts.
Take note of the highway,
  the road you take.
  *Jeremiah 31:21, NIV*

The Journal sections of this book offer you the opportunity to keep a record of your own journey through grief. This is a journey that you have not chosen, but you do have choices in how you respond to your loss. Many people have found in all different kinds of painful situations that writing out their thoughts and feelings is helpful and healing.

During your journey through grief, you will experience many strong and conflicting emotions. Sometimes even your best friends will not be able to really listen to all that you want to tell them. Sometimes you may not be able to speak about what you are feeling. Putting your feelings and experiences on paper acts as a safe method of releasing them. And often the very act of writing provides some distance and perspective on the experience that you otherwise would not have had.

You may think that writing about your loss will not help you feel better soon. And you may be right. Facing a significant loss like a failed pregnancy is painful, and not easily done. It may seem easier not to do it. But the testimony of those who have taken this route before you is that it is necessary to experience the pain, anger, and sadness of the loss before you can move on to healing and acceptance. Writing about it is one way to do this.

There are no right or wrong ways to write about your experience. If you choose to write, please do not feel you should do every Journal section offered. But when you write, consider the following suggestions:

1. Before you begin, choose a notebook that is a size that you find easy to write in. Choose a color that you like. This notebook will be a permanent record of your experience.

2. Every time you write, begin with the date. At a later time the dates will enable you to see the guideposts, the turning points, in your journey through grief.

3. Write as spontaneously as you can. Do not worry about spelling, grammar, and punctuation. Do not be concerned about being "correct."

4. Write honestly. You may be tempted to write how you think you should have felt, rather than how you really felt. You may be ashamed of what you felt, what you said, what you did. In spite of that, try to be as honest as you can.

5. Concentrate on your feelings. Try to identify and describe your feelings as accurately as possible. Use descriptive words and phrases to paint a picture of your feelings at that moment in time.

6. Sometimes it takes a little time to be able to write honestly and deeply about feelings. After selecting the exercise you want to work with, relax and sit quietly. Allow the most important thoughts or feelings to rise to the surface. Then begin writing.

7. Write for yourself. This is your story. At some point you may choose to share portions of the journal with someone else. But consider it personal—your secret and safe place—and write for yourself.

8. Give yourself the freedom to pick and choose the journaling exercises you find meaningful. Do not feel that they all have to be done or that they need to be done in the order presented. Even though there are similarities in sorrow, everyone's grief is different, and there is no set pattern. If at some point none of the questions seem to fit your situation, be your own guide. Write about what is meaningful to you that day.

9. Include in your journal quotes, poems, letters, or scriptures that have moved you and/or encouraged you. They are part of your story.

10. Take *time* to go through the journal exercises. The journey takes time. You may want to spend several days on one exercise. You may find it helpful to return to an earlier exercise and add new thoughts and feelings. You may put the book away for a few weeks, only to get it out and work some more. However you decide to use the journal exercises, give yourself permission to take all the time you need to fully grieve your loss. This is a journey that cannot be hurried.

At times it will seem that the journey is endless and is nothing more than going in circles. Gradually the way will be clearer, and you will feel like there is a future ahead. If you have written about your grief throughout the experience, you will have taken "note of the highway, the road you took." You will be able to look back and see where you have been and the road you have traveled. You will have a record of the suffering, growing, and changing that the journey into grief brought to your life. And someday you will be ready to point out the guideposts for someone else.

# PART ONE

## THE JOURNEY BEGINS

# 1. THIS ISN'T HAPPENING TO ME!

I stared at the darkish blood in disbelief. My final trip to the bathroom before bedtime suddenly became more than routine. What was happening? My pregnancy had been so normal. What did this spotting mean? Was the baby coming early? Surely not—I wasn't ready. All of the undone tasks on my mental list of "Things to Do before Baby Comes" rushed in on me. I fought off rising panic.

Should I call the doctor? The late hour checked me; besides, my eighth-month OB checkup was first thing the next morning. I could talk to him then. I went to bed and prayed that I would not go into labor during the night.

Relief and optimism flooded me as I awoke the next morning with baby intact. I looked forward to my appointment. My husband, Patrick, was going with me to meet the doctor, and I would once again get to hear the baby's heartbeat. I loved hearing the rapid patter fill the room.

My optimism faded slightly when I saw the concern on my doctor's face when I told him about the bleeding the night before. He asked questions and gave me a thorough exam. At its conclusion he said decisively, "I want to send you to Goleta for an ultrasound. You could have placenta previa, and I want to know for sure." Seeing my puzzlement, he explained that sometimes the placenta comes between the baby and cervix and causes spotting.

Patrick and I chatted during the relaxing hour-long drive to Goleta. Our three-year-old son, Travis, sat contentedly between us. The day shimmered with sunshine, and our talk was of the sparkling blue lake and where we would eat lunch. I was excited to be having an ultrasound done. I had been secretly hoping for twins—now I would know for certain.

The hospital was ready for me, and in a short while I was lying on a table next to the ultrasound machine. The congenial technician explained the procedure and squeezed a blob of thick, cold gel onto my baby-filled tummy. Spreading the gel as she went, she methodically moved the probe over every inch of my tummy while I watched the blurry images on the television screen. It was difficult for me to identify what I was seeing, and she helped by saying, "There's a leg. And there's an arm. Right there is the umbilical cord." I was amazed at actually being able to see our baby.

The exam continued on and on as the technician unrelentingly moved the probe. She was a woman about my own age, and we chatted about her six-year-old daughter, my two sons, and my hopes that this baby was a girl. She stopped the exam and took some images to the radiologist. I hoped she was finished. I sighed inwardly when she returned and continued moving the probe. Forty-five minutes crept by, and I wondered what Patrick and Travis were doing; I was anxious to join them for lunch. We needed to get back to Lompoc before Kyle, our first-grade son, got home from school.

Suddenly the baby lurched within me and warm water bathed my legs. My mind spun as I realized what had happened. The technician was oblivious to any change until I stammered, "I don't believe it, but I think my water just broke." She stared at me in disbelief.

She abruptly ended the exam and I went to change back into my clothes. Outwardly I was calm, but my thoughts were racing. I began to formulate a plan: we would go back to Lompoc, I would go to the hospital there, and Patrick would find someone to watch the boys.

A loud pounding on the bathroom door interrupted my thoughts as the radiologist himself came to rush me to the labor room. "Mrs. Morrow, Mrs. Morrow! You need to get on the gurney. We've talked to your doctor and he's agreed we should admit you here." My heart sank. What was going on? Why couldn't I go back to my own doctor? I tried to ignore the urgency in the radiologist's voice as he again urged me to hurry.

Opening the door, I saw that his distraught face matched his voice. He quickly assisted me onto the gurney. I forced myself to form the words I refused to believe. "There's something wrong with the baby, isn't there?" He mumbled a reply about my doctor talking with me soon. I searched his face for reassurance and found none.

Confused thoughts swirled in my head as the gurney jostled down the maze of corridors. "What could possibly be wrong with our baby? I've had no problems with this pregnancy. We have two healthy sons. It must be something minor. Maybe they just don't want me to have the hour-long drive back to my hospital." I refused to think about other possibilities and instead concentrated on watching doors, walls, and white uniforms blur together as we whizzed past.

I knew our destination was close when I spotted a doorway with a sign that read "Birthing Room." Sadness settled in my heart as the dream of having this child in the homey atmosphere of a birthing room was snatched away. Two more turns of the gurney and I was in a labor room.

The next several hours were filled with confusion as people came and went. Patrick took Travis home and made arrangements for the boys' care. I begged him to stay, yet knew he had to go. Aloneness engulfed me, and I squeezed back hot tears as he disappeared through the door.

My new obstetrician came in and introduced himself. I

liked Dr. Corlett immediately. I braced myself as he gently told me the ultrasound test results. "Mrs. Morrow, there appears to be an opening on the baby's spine. We're also seeing something else in the baby's abdominal area that is abnormal, but we can't tell what it is." His words barely penetrated my numbness. My bewildered mind endeavored to form questions, but none came.

I was still reeling from his words when a clerk from admissions came seeking information. Her list of questions seemed endless. I thought she'd never be done. In the other half of the curtained room, another expectant mother struggled to maintain control during contractions. I envied the normalcy of her situation.

I was wheeled to the X-ray department for more pictures. As I lay waiting on the gurney, I struggled to comprehend the doctor's words—"an opening on the baby's spine" and "something else abnormal." My heart resisted accepting his findings. How could two healthy adults have such a child? My thoughts wrestled with each other as I was taken back to my room.

Patrick returned and my relief spilled into tears. I was so glad to have him there to share my disbelief and pain. We had experienced so much joy during the normal deliveries of our sons. Nothing had prepared us to expect anything different this time.

The doctors were in and out during the afternoon, gradually giving us more information. They were puzzled about the abnormality in the abdominal area, but Dr. Corlett was able to tell us that the baby suffered from an "open spine." He discussed with us the disabilities of a child born with this type of problem: paralyzed legs, no control of bladder and bowels—my mind seized the words "paralyzed legs," and I recalled how much quieter this baby had been. Its movements had been so different. My explanation had always been that this baby was a quiet little girl. Now reality edged closer.

Our pastor, Tom, arrived shortly after Patrick returned. He was with us when my doctor came in again and used the phrase "slim chance of survival." The impact of those words took my breath away. The truth suddenly crystallized—our baby was most likely going to die.

## REFLECTION

Judy had many signs that her pregnancy was changing from normal to not normal: her spotting, her doctor's concern, the long ultrasound exam. Yet even when her water broke, her thoughts were to return to her regular doctor and have her baby as originally planned. She could not, would not, believe that something was wrong. Everything would be fine.

Judy's denial of the problem was a natural response. Other women also deny the reality of what is happening to their babies. Carol, for example, kept saying she was fine when bleeding and cramping began in her twelfth week of pregnancy. And Anne put off going to the doctor for a week after miscarrying. She writes, "After my miscarriage on Friday night, I didn't go to the hospital. Weeks before, I had made an appointment for the next Friday with my doctor, and if by some miracle I was still pregnant, I knew I'd find out the truth at that time. In spite of fainting on the bathroom floor, I could not grasp that I really had lost the baby. But the doctor confirmed my worst fears."

Like Judy, Anne and Carol were also denying that something was wrong with their babies. And their reactions were all very normal. Denial—refusing to believe that what is happening is indeed happening—is the mind's way of coping with sudden, unexpected shock. We say, "No! This is not happening to me!" Denial is needed. It gives us time to adjust, to assimilate all that is happening to us.

Judy continued focusing on what she wanted to believe.

But when she was immediately admitted to the hospital,
reality gradually began to slip in. And then she heard those
ominous words: "slim chance of survival."


## JOURNAL

Look back at your pregnancy loss. What were your first
inklings that something was wrong? What did you tell yourself about what was happening? How did you deny what
was happening to you? At what point did the inevitable
become clear to you? What were your feelings then?

# 2. REALITY

In spite of the knowledge that chances of survival were slim, I continued to hope. Different possibilities seesawed in my mind. "Maybe the doctors read the test wrong. Maybe God will choose to heal our baby. Maybe it isn't as disfigured as they think. Maybe the abnormality could be surgically corrected." I clung to every fragment of hope I could think of.

While we waited for labor to begin, Pastor Tom prayed with us and then helped us pass the time by sharing with us his life story, complete with humorous anecdotes. Laughter abounded, and I almost forgot where I was and why I was there, until the baby moved within and jolted me with the truth. And then my heart silently screamed, "This can't be happening! This simply can't be happening to me!"

Tom left about 6:00 P.M. after praying with us again. Before long, I began having mild contractions. Not knowing when he would have another chance, Patrick decided to grab a bite to eat in the cafeteria.

When Patrick returned to the labor room, we shared our fears and concerns. What if the baby did live—could we handle a handicapped child? What caused this abnormality? How should we tell Kyle and Travis? Our families would need to be notified; Pat promised to call them. At times we

9

were silent, lost in our thoughts, still trying to grasp that this nightmare was indeed real.

Now and then the baby moved, and I placed my hands on my stomach, as I had done so often, to capture its movements. Waves of mourning swept over me as I realized we were near the end of our time together. "How incredible," I thought. "This was to have been the beginning, not the end."

As the hours slipped into morning, my labor intensified. I was grateful for the kind words and gentle touch of the night nurse. Soon Dr. Corlett arrived, followed by the anesthesiologist and the pediatrician. I was carefully transferred to the gurney for the short ride to the delivery room. Its green walls and chrome equipment extended a cold greeting. I heaved my bulky shape onto the delivery table. Feet in stirrups, sterilized coverings in place—the stage was set.

Dr. Corlett told me to push and I did. One time, two more —my job was done. I lay back, drained. I listened intently for an infant's cry. The doctor's voice broke the quietness. "The baby had a few heartbeats before dying." My own heart contracted.

"Is it a boy or a girl?" I asked.

"We can't tell due to the abnormality in the abdomen. It doesn't have an abdominal wall."

More shock. "They don't even know if it's a boy or a girl." I struggled to sit up. I had to see this baby I had carried and loved for eight months. The nurse grabbed my shoulders to hold me back. Before she succeeded I caught a glimpse of my child's precious face, so tiny and pale. So perfect. So still. I was struck by the baby's likeness to our two sons as newborns.

The nurse eased me back down to the hard delivery table. The tomblike silence mocked me. No lusty yells echoed from a red-faced newborn. Not even soft indignant whimpers. All prayerful hopes plummeted. Our baby was dead.

## REFLECTION

With a miscarriage or the stillbirth of a child, hopes and dreams come crashing down. You may have had no warning that your labor would not produce a healthy child until the very end. Or you may have had symptoms of impending difficulty for days, all the while hoping and praying that the baby would live. Or you may have discovered, as Judy did, before labor that something was very wrong. In any case, nothing can really prepare you for the grief and disappointment of the final event.

The baby was born—but it didn't live. The miscarriage you hoped to avoid, to prevent, is over. This pregnancy is not going to result in a healthy baby.

Hope and anticipation vanish. The cold, hard reality of death remains. This is the beginning of your journey into grief. Your baby's death is a significant event and worthy of being remembered.

## JOURNAL

Write out the story of your delivery or miscarriage experience. What were your feelings, your physical sensations? Who or what gave you comfort and support?

# 3. THE HOSPITAL EXPERIENCE

My cries tore apart the stillness of the delivery room. Grief ripped my heart in two. Never had I felt such anguish. Wave after wave of pain-filled cries filled the room. I was oblivious to the others in the room. I just knew that someone was crying.

Gradually I became aware of the doctors examining our baby's body. I realized that Patrick was stroking my hair, trying to ease my pain. And I realized that those loud wails I was hearing were coming from me. I became self-conscious and tried to stifle my tears. I mumbled an apology to the nurse. She encouraged me to cry, saying, "Don't hold back. Cry all you want. You need to get it out."

It wasn't long before I was back on the familiar gurney, traveling through the seemingly endless hospital corridors. A few sobs continued to escape, and I wondered if I would ever get to my room. Were they taking me as far away from my baby as they possibly could?

When we finally got to my room, I was thankful that I was not close to the hospital nursery. I cringed at the thought of hearing healthy newborns crying. I was relieved that I had a room to myself. Once the nurse had settled me into my bed, Patrick and I were momentarily alone. He sat beside me and I fell into his arms. As we held each other close, our tears flowed together. Shock and disbelief were mirrored on our faces. Surely we would wake up soon and this nightmare would end.

Another nurse entered the room with questions about taking care of the baby's body. Dr. Corlett had told us in the delivery room that he was going to record the birth as a stillbirth, even though the baby had had a few heartbeats, because then the hospital would take care of the body. That sounded reasonable to us and we agreed. The nurse informed us that the doctor was new to this hospital and was not aware of the hospital's policy that any baby over twenty weeks was the parents' responsibility. She told us about a mortuary a few blocks from the hospital that would cremate a baby's body for twenty-five dollars. We mechanically nodded our heads, "That would be fine."

It was now long past the 2:00 A.M. time of birth, and Patrick and I were both exhausted. Patrick stretched out on the extra bed in my room. A nurse kept coming in to check my vital signs. Each time she woke me, I remembered what had happened. I resented her intrusions, yet I knew she was only doing her job. At one point, she told me how sorry she was about my loss and shared that she, too, had lost a baby when she was about six months pregnant. It helped to know that she understood.

Patrick left early in the morning to take care of the children. Later Dr. Corlett came in to examine me. After determining that I could be released, he slumped down in the bedside chair. His obvious dejection at our loss touched me. But I felt responsible for his sadness, as though my failure to produce a normal child had caused him to feel that he had somehow failed.

I wanted to make him feel better, so I talked brightly and assured him that I was doing just fine. I glibly told him that I was sure there was a purpose in all this. He mumbled that he was glad I was able to feel that way, said good-bye, and quietly left my room.

I put on the same maternity clothes that I had worn to the

hospital. Was it only yesterday? How quickly everything had changed. I sat in a daze and distractedly watched TV while I waited for Patrick to come. It all seemed so unreal. I felt a stab of pain when I saw a diaper commercial. But mostly I felt numb.

When Patrick arrived to take me home, Pastor Tom was with him. They had obviously enjoyed visiting with each other during the drive and were in good spirits. Their jovial moods increased my sense of disbelief. Did our baby really die?

I was jarred back to reality when the nurse brought in the customary wheelchair to take me out to the car. Immediately the memories of taking our two sons home from the hospital swept over me. Suddenly I was there again— joyfully dressing them in their first tiny clothing, carefully wrapping them in receiving blankets and proudly holding them in my arms as I was wheeled out of the hospital, reveling in the comments of people passing by.

And now—nothing. The small "coming home from the hospital" outfit would never clothe this baby. There were no indications of "new mother." I looked pretty much like any other patient. There was no cause for exclamations or conversation from admiring strangers. As I was wheeled out to the car, pain washed over me anew. I swallowed back fresh tears. There was no joy here, only sorrow. I was going home without my baby. My arms were painfully empty.

## REFLECTION

Anyone experiencing pregnancy loss has to deal with people in the medical profession. Some are compassionate, caring, knowledgeable, sympathetic. Others are cold, insensitive, inexperienced, and unable to deal with your loss. In many ways, except for your initial choice of doctor, you have little control over the people you come in contact with at the time of your loss. However, their actions, their responses to you, are part of the story and often part of the grief of pregnancy loss.

Judy felt she received compassionate care even though she did not know the doctor who delivered her baby. The nurses were helpful and supportive. They encouraged her to cry and to express her grief. They expressed sympathy for her.

Judy's hospital experience was probably about average for someone experiencing miscarriage or stillbirth. Some hospitals excel at giving supportive help at such times. Others, unfortunately, are dismal failures. Most fall somewhere in between.

Judy later realized that she had been deprived of any opportunity to see or hold her baby. She caught a brief glimpse of its face, but she was never given the opportunity to say hello or good-bye to this much-wanted child. She and Patrick were also not given adequate time to really think about what they wanted done with the baby's body. Instead, the one choice presented made them feel it was a problem that needed to be quickly disposed of.

Betsy's experience was much different. Betsy had carried her baby past term when he died in the womb. She entered the hospital on Sunday morning to have labor induced, knowing already that her baby would be stillborn. She writes:

> They started the pitocin around 9:00 A.M. Sunday, but contractions didn't become uncomfortable until around 9:00 P.M. when active labor began. At 7:00 Monday morning they decided to turn off the pitocin. I was only three and a half centimeters dilated and the baby's head was not moving down.
>
> At this point, they decided to do a C-section, and I was in the operating room within an hour. I remember the anesthetist saying he was sorry this wasn't a "normal" C-section. When I came to, I was asking Jim if it was a girl or a boy, and he told me it was a boy.

They wheeled me back to my room, and Jim came walking down the hall with this blue bundle. I still felt joy seeing Jim carry our son. I lay on my side and Jim placed him in my arms. Baby James looked so beautiful. His hair was wet and looked wavy. His little hands were long and delicate. It was such a miracle to at last see this tiny human whom I had carried for nine months, and who came from our love for each other. I wanted to take him home. I kissed him on the forehead and gave him back to Jim. It was a bittersweet moment.

The nurses came in and weighed and measured James. They took a picture of Jim holding our son. Jim took a picture of James and me. These pictures are some of my most valued possessions.

I spent the next five days concentrating on getting well enough to leave the hospital for James's memorial service. I left the hospital on Friday and felt my hospital stay was as good as it could have been. Everyone was so compassionate and caring.

Cathie's experience was different from Judy's and Betsy's. She entered the hospital in labor, expecting to deliver a healthy baby, her second child. In the previous few months, her house had burned to the ground, and her husband had been hospitalized with a severe viral infection. So although pregnant, she had not been giving the coming baby a lot of thought. But as labor started, she began to really anticipate the birth of the baby. She writes:

The joy of having a little newborn again to hold and nurse finally hit me. I was actually excited. I sat in the labor room working through the contractions and waiting for the doctor on call to come in. I waited for over an hour—it seemed like forever. He asked where Craig was because he had some bad news for us. Craig had only been out of the hospital for five days and was home resting, so I told him he could tell me, never thinking it was anything more serious than that they might send me home because my labor wasn't strong enough or that they needed to do a C-section.

Instead he told me that my baby had a serious head problem and probably wouldn't live an hour. He said he was sorry and left.

First I sat in shock. Then I called Craig and told him I needed him back at the hospital. My friend, Gail, who was supporting me through labor, prayed with me. Craig came and I managed to tell him, and he in turn had to break the news to the rest of the family.

Gail stayed with me during the rest of the labor. When delivery time came, I went in alone. A few pushes and the baby was out. The nurse attending covered my eyes, but I didn't want to look. They whisked my baby out of the room wrapped in a blanket. The doctor sewed me up and I was taken back to the labor room.

The next few hours are a blur. I stayed in the labor room all night—crying, awake, unable to sleep. One nurse walked in in the middle of the night and hugged me. I will never forget that. I could hear babies crying in the delivery room, and I wondered if my baby had died yet.

The next morning I showered and was anxious to leave. But I had to wait and wait to see a doctor. I wanted to see the OB doctor, and I also really wanted to see my son's pediatrician. When the OB doctor came in, Craig was there and asked him what people in our situation usually do. He told us that most parents have an autopsy done, let the hospital dispose of the body, and put an announcement in the paper. We thought that sounded like the easiest thing to do to help us forget and go on. I didn't think I wanted a lot of "fuss."

After what seemed like an eternity, the pediatrician finally came in. I was desperate for information about the baby. He told me it was a boy and that his problem wasn't anencephaly as the obstetrician had thought. Instead my baby had a rare problem known as amniotic bands malformation. He told me this was not genetic, but it is a problem caused by the rupture of the inside layer of the amniotic sac early in pregnancy, and that no one knows what causes the rupture.

I felt some better after talking to the pediatrician, but before I left the hospital I had to undergo the torture of being asked by well-meaning but uninformed people about birth and death certificates, nursing the baby, and baby pictures.

The next thing I remember is leaving the hospital with empty arms. Other new mothers had their babies. I couldn't wait to get out of there. I just wanted to run away from the pain. We left the hospital knowing that our baby was alone, isolated, and dying.

The baby lived for six days—some of the worst days of my life. I hated to go anywhere because I didn't want to see anyone. Trying to put the baby behind us, we told all but the closest of family that the baby was stillborn. On one of my rare trips outside the house, my friend and I ran into one of her pregnant friends. I had to leave their presence. I began to realize then that I was not going to be able to run away from my pain.

Five days after the birth, I felt compelled to go to the hospital to be with my baby. My pediatrician met me there, and we talked in the physicians' lounge. He did not think I should see the baby and told me they were doing nothing to keep him alive; in fact, the baby was showing signs of failing. The doctor drew pictures for me, to show me what was wrong with him. He was kind, but actually not very understanding of my need to see and hold my child. The next day while we were eating dinner, the doctor called to tell me that the baby had died.

Cathie experienced a lot of pain in the hospital because doctors and nurses were not sensitive to her needs. She felt let down by the doctors. She certainly was not encouraged to fully face the pain of her loss while she was there. Instead they sent her home, never having seen this baby she was so anticipating.

Women who experience losses earlier in pregnancy are also sometimes less than happy with their hospital experience. One woman who had been spotting all the previous day was finally given an appointment for 9:00 the next morning. She writes:

Never have I felt such a restrained and detached manner as I did that morning with the nurse who examined me. She said my cervix was closed, that there was a fifty-fifty chance things were all right, and that I should take it easy and not have sex. All I wanted to have was a baby, to know that things would be all right. She also admonished me for my busy schedule, my running, and for not eating enough.[1]

Later, when it became obvious this woman was going to miscarry, she returned to the hospital.

There was a long wait at the emergency room and many dull, plodding questions. The cold and efficient doctor jammed the speculum against my cervix as I writhed in pain.

"Yes, you are miscarrying," was her cold pronouncement. "We'll have to do a curettage."

I blurted a bunch of questions: "Are you sure?" and "Why?" and "What will you do?" I could not keep back my tears. "Can you run some tests?" I asked, remembering the business about "collecting the fetus."

"No, we only run tests when a woman has had three miscarriages."

Three miscarriages! I couldn't believe it. You mean someone has to go through this three times before it's taken seriously?

But before I could become too outraged, or feel my impending grief very much, they started anesthesia.

The curettage was nothing compared to the pain and agony of the whole day. I was in a slippery consciousness, a wet fog of nowhereness, and only in the very back of my mind did I know or grapple with the fact that we had lost our baby.

\* \* \* \*

"You have reached the advice nurse for ob-gyn. Your call will be taken in the order received."

[1]Marian McDonald, "Miscarriage: The Silent Wail," *Birth Stories: The Experience Remembered,* ed. Janice Isaacs Ashford (Trumansburg, NY: The Crossing Press, 1984), p. 142. Used by permission of the author.

The wait for the advice nurse never seemed so long as on the day, two days after the miscarriage, when all of a sudden the inevitable grief of losing our much-wanted baby hit me. I felt so deeply grieved, so pained, I did not know if I would survive. I had lost something, someone, so very close, so very intimate, that I felt I had lost a part of myself.

"I have just had a miscarriage and I would like to talk with someone about how I'm feeling about my grief," I said to the nurse.

"What?" she asked, "You want to have an abortion?"

"No, I had a miscarriage, and I want to talk with someone."

"Well, how far along are you? When do you want to have the abortion?"

"NURSE, I HAD A MISCARRIAGE, I LOST MY BABY!!!"

I was dumbfounded at the insensitivity. Didn't she realize it was hard enough for me to say those words once, let alone three times?

Finally she got it and said, "I'll switch you to psychiatry."

But I didn't want someone in psychiatry! I didn't need a shrink! I just needed someone who knew what I was going through, who could walk through some of it with me, who could tell me I wasn't going to feel like this forever.[2]

Even if the care and consideration in the hospital are excellent, few women are sent home with any forewarning of the grief that is to follow. Judy certainly had no warning that this experience of loss was so important—one worthy of mourning. She needed to know that this loss would require the pain and work of grieving, and was not one that she would be over in a few days or even weeks. No one told her though, and she left the hospital with empty arms, an aching heart, and a determination to get life back to normal as soon as possible.

[2]Ibid., 143–144.

## JOURNAL

What was your overall feeling about your hospital experience? Who was compassionate? Who was not? Who made you angry? Did you express that anger to them? If not, what do you wish you had said? What would you like to tell that person now?

How did you feel about your own behavior? Were you embarrassed by your lack of control? How did the doctors and nurses respond to you?

Were you given choices about what was happening? Were you asked if you wanted to see the baby? Were you given options for making arrangements for the body? What did you do? How do you feel about it? If you had this part of your experience to live over again, what would you like to do differently?

What were your feelings as you left the hospital? Were you warned that there were still hard times ahead?

# 4. COMING HOME

Still in a state of emotional numbness, I sat eating lunch in the Santa Barbara sunshine with Patrick and Tom. The pleasant outdoor cafe invited laughter and conversation—a sharp contrast to the events of the previous twenty-four hours. It all seemed so incongruous. There were moments when I forgot what had just happened. Yet each time I remembered, the knife of grief dug deeper and I hurt more.

Our bantering continued on the drive home, but as we approached Lompoc my heart grew heavier and heavier. We dropped Tom off at his house and drove on to pick up our two sons. Tears welled up in my eyes just thinking about trying to tell them. I pictured them with their dark brown hair and big blue eyes and wondered how they would react. They had been excited about a new baby joining our family. Patrick and I agreed that we would wait until we got home before we told them the sad news.

I was thankful the drive home with the boys was only a few blocks. Our oldest son, Kyle, punctuated the short drive with one question, "Where's the baby? Where's the baby?" In his excitement and anticipation, he didn't notice my tears and silence. Then he concluded, "I know, the baby's in the little baby bed in the house." When we pulled up in the driveway, he jumped out of the car and ran in the house and straight to the nursery. He came running out seconds later with a puzzled expression and demanded again, "Where's the baby?"

By this time I was crying steadily. Patrick pulled both boys up on his lap and gently explained that the baby had died. At three, Travis didn't totally comprehend Patrick's words and seemed somewhat confused. He reflected our sorrow, however, as he looked at Patrick and then at me with a wide-eyed, sad look.

Kyle understood immediately and was terribly upset. He started crying and lamented again and again, "But I didn't even get to see the baby. I didn't even get to see the baby." Pain filled his voice and distorted his six-year-old face. His deep disappointment and grief pierced me with new pain.

That evening Patrick returned to work, so a friend came to stay with me. Other friends had brought in dinner, so my friend Mary did the dishes and straightened the house. After tucking the kids in bed, Mary and I sat in the living room together and talked.

Several years earlier Mary's first child had died in her womb during her seventh month of pregnancy. It was several weeks later before she delivered.

In many ways I felt like Mary understood what I was going through. Yet I was also disturbed by some of her comments. I squirmed inside when she related how relieved she was when she finally delivered her baby. She had been almost impatient when others expressed sympathy, because she wanted to get on with her life. More than anything she felt relief.

I felt like she expected me to feel the same way. I knew that Pastor Tom had told her earlier how serene I was when the doctors gave us the news and how well I was doing. I didn't want to say or do anything that would not live up to her expectations. I wanted to continue to "do well."

So in my numbness, tiredness, and not wanting to make waves, I nodded my head and acted as if I agreed with what Mary was saying. Inwardly I protested. "Relief? I don't feel relief! I feel terrible pain. I can't believe this has happened to me. I wasn't prepared for this. How can you expect me to feel relief?"

By bedtime I was emotionally drained and still physically tired from the entire experience. I assured Mary I would be fine and insisted that she go home and be with her family. She offered several times to stay overnight with me, but I sent her home. I knew I was exhausted enough to sleep.

My continued shock and numbness dictated the factual diary entry I made late that night.

Midnight. Our baby died this morning right after I delivered it. Not even sure if it was a boy or girl. It didn't even have an abdominal wall and had a sac on its spinal cord. Got a few hours sleep, so did Pat. He went back to Lompoc and then he and Tom came later and picked me up. Folks, Becky, and Nancy called. Mary was here all evening. I'm so tired.

Then I crawled into bed and automatically placed my hands on my tummy to feel the baby's movements. My hands recoiled as the reality of our loss touched my fingertips. More tears in the darkness, then sleep came.


## REFLECTION

After you lose a baby through miscarriage or stillbirth, your family and friends have to be told. Even as your mind and body are trying to assimilate all that has happened, you must tell others what you yourself don't completely understand.

If you already have children, they too will feel disappointed. They will also feel your sadness. And the pain they feel will add to your own pain.

Telling parents, brothers and sisters, and friends offers you the opportunity to express once again the reality of what happened. But the telling also brings pain once more

—this really happened . . . our baby really died. What seemed so unbelievable, so much like a bad dream, becomes more and more real.

Friends and relatives will probably respond in love, although some may literally not know what to say or do. They may feel the pain of your loss, but ultimately, you will be alone with your grief and pain.

## JOURNAL

Who did you come home to? Who did you first tell about what had happened? How did they respond? Did you feel a need to "do well" or be strong? If you could relive that day what would you do or say differently?

If you have children, what did you tell them? How did they respond? How did this make you feel?

What was it like to go to bed that first night at home? Write about how you felt.

# PART TWO

---

# THE FIRST FEW DAYS

# 5. EMPTINESS

Emptiness. Sheer emptiness. It was as if a vacuum had sucked every fragment of vitality from my body. No life squirming within me, no warm bundle nestled in my arms. Just emptiness.

I was numb. It seemed so unreal. It was almost as if I had not been pregnant at all. Yet the overwhelming emptiness was a constant reminder. I felt as if a chasm had been carved in my womb. A relentless chant marched through my mind: "Empty womb, empty arms; empty womb, empty arms." At times it was a forlorn whisper; at other times the words screamed with pain. "Empty, empty, empty."

My arms literally ached with emptiness. From my wrists to above the elbows, they ached for weeks. I rubbed my arms to ease the pain, to erase the longing to hold my child. Rubbing did not help. The aching persisted. I felt so strange, so abnormal. Had anyone else experienced such pain, such emptiness?

Two weeks after our baby's death, I attended a church dinner. The out-of-town speaker had brought with him his wife and their eight-week-old baby daughter. At first I eyed the baby from afar, but her tiny form drew me to her. I eagerly offered to hold her so her mother could go through the buffet line. I held their sweet baby girl with great intensity,

29

hoping that doing so would relieve the pain in my arms. It did not. My arms continued to ache, yearning for the weight of my child, the child I had carried. I felt so empty.

## REFLECTION

As the emotional numbness wore off, Judy experienced intense feelings of emptiness. Her body no longer nurtured life and her arms had no baby to hold. Her arms actually ached to hold that baby.

An intense feeling of emptiness is a normal response to the loss of a baby. Even at the conclusion of a normal pregnancy, many women experience sadness at the pregnancy's ending. For months the unborn child has been such an intimate part of the mother's life. Now mother and child are no longer so close physically. But that loss is overshadowed by the presence of the new baby that is there to be held, loved, and taken care of.

When a pregnancy ends unexpectedly with the loss of a child, the grief over the loss is unrelieved by a child in your arms. Suddenly not only is your body empty, your whole life seems consumed by emptiness. Like Judy, Kim and Betsy also experienced feelings of emptiness in the weeks following pregnancy loss.

Kim's first pregnancy ended with the premature birth of a son who lived for only two hours. In her words: "The house was hollow of warmth. Music sounded empty. The radio only made noise. Nothing could fill the emptiness that hung like wet, cold fog." And two weeks after Betsy's son was stillborn, she wrote:

> I seem to be feeling a little stronger—emotionally. The tears have come a little less frequently in the last two days. It seems I can now do daily tasks and not have our loss of James be my most conscious thought. But even when I'm not consciously mourning him, there is an ache in my heart—a heartache or emptiness.

Judy's feelings of emptiness and grief actually manifested themselves physically in the aching of her arms. She did not know that this is a response that other women have also experienced—that it is not abnormal. Pregnancy loss is a shock experienced both emotionally and physically. Profound fatigue, difficulty sleeping, loss of appetite, and unexplained aches such as Judy's aching arms are all common physical symptoms of grief.

Kim's arms didn't ache, but she remembers feeling tired all the time. Paradoxically, she also had trouble sleeping at night. She writes:

> I couldn't sleep. I had nightmares. I heard every noise, creak, or groan in the house. I would finally fall asleep only to be wakened by the phone. It was six weeks before I could sleep six or seven hours straight.
>
> I felt totally exhausted, even right after getting up from a nap or a night's rest. It was an effort to move, to shower, to dress, to think, to do anything. By the end of the first week, I felt better for about fifteen minutes after a nap or after eating. It was two or three months before I could go a whole day without a nap.

Grief is painful. The emptiness may seem overwhelming. You may feel like you're living in a body you hardly know anymore. It's no longer nurturing a baby; you have nothing to hold in your arms. Exhausted, you can't sleep. Nothing feels right. You may feel like the emptiness will never be filled.

## JOURNAL

What word best describes your feelings in the days and weeks after your loss? When did you feel this way the most? Did you think that your feelings were strange or abnormal? Did you experience any physical manifestations of your grief? What were they?

# 6. SILENCED LULLABIES

The baby's nursery silently greeted me when I arrived home from the hospital—another jolting reminder of my loss. The wicker bassinet was ready to cradle our baby. The white crib stood nearby, where we'd set it up when we'd moved into the house two months earlier. The yellow and white gingham window mini-blinds were on order. Newly washed miniature clothing lay neatly folded in the drawers. The arms of the rocking chair stretched out in anticipation.

Everything indicating "baby" had found its niche in that room; calling it "the nursery" had come naturally. Just going in there had quickened my heartbeat and my sense of expectancy. I had often pictured our newborn curled up in bed. I had played with the tiny clothes, unfolding them and folding them again, imagining their softness enfolding my child. Lullabies had run through my head.

Now the nursery was a constant reminder of my loss. Even with the door closed, its silence and emptiness haunted me. To dispel the hurt, I wanted to pack away anything that said "baby" and rid our home of it forever. My wise mom gently counseled me, "Judy, why don't you just pack up everything and store it out in the garage for awhile? You'll be better able to decide what to do with it in a few months."

Her suggestion made sense to me and inwardly I was relieved. As much as I desired no reminders of my loss, another part of me wanted to wrap my arms around all of it and never let go.

Mom offered to help me pack the baby things before she returned to Oregon, so one afternoon we set about the task. I dreaded it. I feared I would lose control completely and soak each little sleeper with my tears. I resolved to be in control. Mom and I purposely made small talk while we transferred the clothing from drawers to cardboard boxes. I resisted the urge to hold up each item and cry with new mourning for the child who would never wear them. My heart ached with fresh pain.

Eventually we turned that room into a den and moved the TV in there. However, habit had etched the term *nursery* into our vocabulary as the designation for that room, and the word pricked my heart each time one of us forgot.

## REFLECTION

Part of the anticipation of pregnancy is getting ready to take care of the baby's physical needs. Clothes and furniture are bought, borrowed, received as gifts, or taken out of storage. A place is prepared for this new child—a place for sleeping, eating, playing, and loving.

In early pregnancy, the evidence that a baby is coming is often seen in the books on the nightstand or end table— books on pregnancy, childbirth, child care, and child development. Books of names and lists of possible choices add to the stack. And even in the early months, plans are made for the changes that will need to take place with the arrival of this baby. Mentally the furniture is rearranged and lists of things needed are made.

Then the pregnancy fails, and there is no baby for the nursery. All of the preparation and anticipation was for nothing. Facing the empty nursery or even the pile of books is painful.

Some women ask someone else to remove these things for them before they come home from the hospital. That way they come home to a house where all traces of the expected baby have been removed.

Others choose to leave the nursery standing and the baby things ready, in the hope that the next pregnancy will succeed and that a baby will live in that room. One woman who suffered several pregnancy losses before two successful pregnancies kept a nursery ready for several years. She commented, "Some of the diapers we bought the first time lost the stick-um before we could use them . . ."

Others have found that dismantling the nursery, putting away the books, is a painful process, but one that helps them recognize the finality of this loss. Packing the baby things away becomes part of the work of grief and part of the process of healing. One mother who miscarried shares how putting the things away was healing for her.

> Jorge suggested we gather all the baby books and other items and put them away together. He prepared an altar and set the tone for a prayer service. That evening proved to be the most meaningful way we had of expressing our grief.[1]

Putting the baby things away, shutting the nursery door, are ways of stepping into the reality of a pregnancy loss. The preparations for this baby have to be stopped. There may be hopes for future babies, but these hopes are tempered by the knowledge that a pregnancy does not guarantee a healthy baby. And hope for the future, symbolized by the ready nursery and the tiny clothes, does not take away the pain of the loss of this particular child.

[1]© February 1986, "Marriage: Remnants of a Life," by Mary Davis. Reprinted with permission from *Marriage and Family Living* magazine (pp. 15–16), Abbey Press. Saint Meinrad Arch Abbey, Saint Meinrad, IN 47577.

## JOURNAL

Describe the nursery you had prepared or were preparing for your baby. What was your favorite thing for this baby—a gift from someone special, a favorite toy, a blanket, a handmade cradle? Tell about it.

What did you choose to do with the nursery, the books, the baby things? If you packed things away, how did you feel while doing it? How did you act? (Did you, like Judy, act much differently than the way you were actually feeling?) If you had to make the decision today, would you handle the baby things in the same way? Why or why not?

# 7. ADDING INSULT TO INJURY

My body refused to acknowledge that my baby died. My milk came in at the appropriate time. My doctor did not want to give me medication to dry it up because of the small danger of blood clots. Instead, he suggested using ice packs to alleviate the swelling, but they did little to help.

As my breasts enlarged with useless milk, my sorrow increased in like measure. I had nursed both my sons and knew what a relief it was to put a suckling infant to a milk engorged breast. Now the pain taunted me; there was no nursing baby to relieve it.

My milk would often "let down" during the day. At home I would press my arms against my breasts to stop the flow and ease the uncomfortable tingling sensation. When having lunch out with Mom, I refrained from doing this, only to discover a large wet spot on my blouse. Frustration and embarrassment overwhelmed me.

Accustomed to sleeping on my side, I now had to lie on my back. In this position I awoke often and would remember anew what had happened. My body had betrayed me. First it produced an inadequate child, and now it mocked me by providing milk for a child who didn't live.

In addition to the unnecessary milk, my sagging skin and rounded form were also constant reminders of my failed pregnancy. There was no child in my arms to explain my still rounded body. My normal clothes refused to fit, and I had come to loathe my maternity clothes. Earlier I had worn them with joyful anticipation. Now they hung on me lifelessly. They were painful reminders of what was to be and what was not.

All the discomforts I had endured during pregnancy now seemed so unfair and so needless. Painful varicose veins had plagued me the last two months of the pregnancy, particularly in the area by my left ankle. When I had gotten up at night, the ripping pain had been so severe I could barely walk. During the day I had worn white surgical hose that encased my legs from the top of my thighs to my toes. Every morning I had struggled to get into them before swinging my legs out of bed.

Besides the varicose veins, in mid-pregnancy I had suffered from a pinched nerve in my hip. At times I could not find a comfortable position standing, sitting, or lying down. Now in my loss I remembered the time when the pain in my hip and leg was so severe that I rolled around on the floor, desperately trying to find a position that did not hurt.

Now the unneeded milk, the sagging skin, the stretch marks, the varicose veins, and the discomfort I had endured were painful reminders of what I did not have. With a baby in my arms, these physical discomforts would have been easily minimized. Now they seemed like a high price to pay for a broken heart.

## REFLECTION

The dramatic changes that take place in a woman's body following pregnancy are often difficult and uncomfortable. The new mother experiences the discomfort of milk coming in and letting down, and struggles to get into her pre-pregnancy clothes. She is sometimes beset by postpartum depression. For most women this trying time is made

easier because there is a reward—a baby to love, hold, and
nurture.

For the woman whose pregnancy ends in loss, these
changes are much harder to bear. You discover, much to
your chagrin, that your body does not know that the baby
you recently delivered did not live. With no baby in your
arms, you find yourself living in a body that is preparing to
nurture a baby.

This seems shocking and unfair, but it is nonetheless
true. However, it can help to know that others have similar
feelings. Cathie writes:

> It was like there was a short-circuit in my brain. I knew I
> had had a baby. My breasts were leaking. I was fat and
> I was still a little weak, but there was no baby.

And Kim says:

> Because of my stage in pregnancy (twenty-five weeks)
> and all the liquid I was drinking, my milk came in full blast. I
> could have nursed twins with ease. This only added insult to
> injury. I figured the least God could have done was decrease
> my milk supply. It took two weeks for it to finally dry up.

For the woman whose baby does not live, the whole pregnancy with its discomforts and inconveniences may seem in
retrospect to have been an exercise in futility. Why did you
have to endure the mood swings, the nausea, the tiredness
—all the changes—if it was to come to nothing? Why did
you eat so carefully and take such good care of yourself if it
weren't going to do any good?

When pregnancy ends with a normal, healthy child, the
physical changes, discomforts, and sacrifices seem a small
price to pay. When, however, the pregnancy ends in the
death of the child, the post-pregnancy changes and the
memories of the pregnancy itself are painful reminders of
an anticipated joy that is now lost.

## JOURNAL

Describe your pregnancy. How did you feel physically? Did you resent or welcome the changes in your body? How did you feel emotionally? Did you have special joys in being pregnant? (Although sorrow may now overshadow any joy you had during your pregnancy, those pleasures are part of your story, too.)

Did you make special sacrifices to bring this pregnancy to term? Did you experience pain and discomfort? Are there permanent changes in your body because of this pregnancy? Do you feel bitterness, anger, or resentment because of what you endured?

How did your body respond after your baby was born? Did any of these changes make you particularly angry or upset? Write about it.

# 8. THE WORST DAY: BABIES EVERYWHERE

Three days after our baby's death, postpartum depression attacked. Its heavy gloom threatened to suffocate me. "This isn't fair!" I silently protested. "I'm barely handling my grief; I don't need anything else."

It was Saturday. I tried to shed the cloak of depression that I felt wrapping itself around me. Mom and I were going shopping, and I didn't want to spoil our time together.

It seemed so unreal and absurd. I loved to shop with Mom, but this visit was not meant for that pastime. We were supposed to be changing tiny diapers and trading off shoulders for that last stubborn burp. We had expected to be admiring delicate fingers and toes, bathing petal-soft skin, and searching for smile dimples. (Mom had taken great delight in being the first to find our sons' dimples.)

Instead of taking care of a baby, we went shopping. My heart wasn't in it. It was depressing to try on clothes over my still bulky body. I bought a gray sweater. It matched my mood.

On the way home we stopped by a garage sale. We poked around, looking for treasures. Another family arrived and the woman running the sale greeted them enthusiastically. "Did you hear about my new grandbaby?"

she asked. Excitedly she told her friends about her new grandson, born a few days earlier. Bubbling with joy, she shared all the details.

As she spoke, my pain enlarged and inside I wept. I wanted to cry out to her and the world, "I had a baby, too! I had a baby, too! And this is *my* baby's grandma." My heart thudded to my toes as I once again faced the painful truth. "But my baby died. My baby died."

A fresh wave of sadness and depression swept over me as we drove home. Suddenly I no longer felt capable of maintaining control and handling my loss well. My bravery crumbled like a deserted sand castle. At home I continued to feel out of sorts, barely able to get through the remainder of the day. I grumped at the boys for trivial offenses and then hated myself for doing it.

Early in the evening I was sorting the boys' clothes, trying to find them outfits for church the next day. I glanced out the front window to see a couple slowly walking by. The man was cradling a newborn infant in his arms. The woman was wearing a smocked top. It was obvious she had just had a baby.

I immediately burst into tears and cried inconsolably. Pain assaulted me with new intensity. It was almost unbearable. And entwined with the pain was overwhelming confusion. Why did our baby die and why did their baby live? Why? Why? Why?

I went to bed thinking it had been the worst day yet. There were newborns bringing joy to everyone else, but not to us. Numbness was wearing off and unrelenting pain was setting in.

## REFLECTION

You are no longer pregnant. There is no baby. Suddenly your life has been turned upside down. And even more suddenly you may feel like you are surrounded by pregnant

women or women with new babies. There are babies everywhere.

Coming to terms with the babies and pregnant women
around you is part of the grief work of pregnancy loss. Not
facing your pain at this point can lead to damaged relationships. Anne shares her experience:

> Two weeks after my miscarriage, we visited friends in
> another city. They had just welcomed their third child, a
> darling little boy, home from the hospital. I went through
> all the right motions and said all the right things, but I
> couldn't bring myself to pick him up. In the following
> weeks I backed away from that friendship until the weeks
> grew into months and then to years. I had excuses for my
> actions, but the truth was I couldn't bear for her to have
> another baby. I felt so left out.

Landie's experience, though similar, had a different outcome. Two days after her loss of a baby in her sixth month
of pregnancy, Landie ran into two pregnant friends in the
grocery store. She writes:

> Anger, bitterness, and self-pity started to well up and
> overtake me. I thought I'd faint—my emotions were suffo-
> cating me. My friends turned away from me in fear. They
> knew of my loss and didn't know how to continue in their
> own joy.
>
> I knew there would be no healing for me if we did not
> bridge this insurmountable gap. I turned up their aisle with
> shaky legs and tears in my eyes. I said, "Debby, Audrey, it's
> OK. I'm doing fine. How are you?" We cried and shared with
> each other—fear, anger, joy, and love. I was able to go on and
> enjoy their new babies, and ten years later we're still closely
> bonded friends.

Landie summoned up the courage to face the pain of her
friends' continued and successful pregnancies. But it wasn't
easy.

Facing the pain that comes from seeing other babies and pregnant women takes time and work. Kim says that she hated pregnant women or women with small babies for at least a month after her loss. She also hated their complacency—their seeming assumption that babies come easily, naturally, and when planned. And she hated the fact that these women were unaware of her pain. They were blissfully unaware and happy, and she was so sad.

As Judy did, you may find yourself questioning the fairness of other women having healthy babies when you did not. Judy was intensely angry and jealous. It may be difficult for you to admit how angry and jealous you are. Your feelings may seem ugly and harsh. You may not want to admit the deep hurt you feel.

Intense anger at life's unfairness and intense jealousy of women with babies are normal responses at this point. Your loss is real and your pain is also very real. Admitting and facing these feelings is an important part of your journey.

## JOURNAL

When and where did you see your first pregnant woman or newborn child after your loss? How did you feel? What did you do?

Has your loss affected your relationship with friends who are pregnant or those who have young babies? How have you acted around them? How have they responded to your loss?

# 9. TRYING TO MAKE SENSE OF IT

The week after my baby's death, my mind simmered with questions and confusion. "There has to be a significant reason for this," I told myself. I decided if I could discover the reason behind this personal tragedy of mine, maybe the pain would be more bearable. My mind groped for an answer, any answer.

During this time, one image kept coming to me: I could see our family on a ship that capsized. A rescue boat came near. The ominous words of the rescuer rang in my ears. "There's room for four—no more."

In my confusion and grief, I decided a situation like that could happen. And I concluded that the message for me was that there was only room for four in our family.

I remember sitting on the couch with my mom and telling her about the ship at sea and that there was room for four—no more. She solemnly nodded her head and listened with understanding and caring. She didn't tell me I was silly or crazy. She seemed to realize that, although my thinking was not rational, it was part of my struggle to find some sense and meaning in the event.

I felt somehow responsible for my baby's death. I meticulously reviewed each month of my pregnancy, looking for the smallest clue to resolve the whys. Question after question plagued me. Did I take any medication that could have caused this? Did I work too hard during our move? Was I on my feet too much? Had my diet been adequate? None of my questions had conclusive answers, which left me even more frustrated.

I wondered why I had not miscarried early in the pregnancy since the baby had so many defects. I was amazed that I had carried the baby for eight months. And I was angry that I hadn't miscarried. If it had to happen, why did I have to go through all those months of joyful anticipation?

My doctor assured me that for some unknown reason something had gone wrong in the early weeks of my pregnancy. He emphasized that it was not my fault, that it was just a baffling "fluke of nature." I, however, kept trying to find a cause, a reason. I wanted something to blame this tragedy on. Somehow that would make it easier to bear. But I could not find the reason. Even in that I failed.

## REFLECTION

When faced with an inexplicable loss, our minds eventually try to fill the void. Where there are no explanations, it seeks to provide an explanation; where there are no answers, it seeks to provide answers.

Judy's mind provided her with the image of a rescue boat with room for four—no more. This image was in no way a rational explanation. But somehow the idea that there was room for only four in the Morrow family seemed to make sense.

Her other response was decidedly more rational and analytic, although it began with the irrational premise that the loss was her fault. She decided to find out exactly what she had done wrong. She reviewed her every action during the pregnancy, looking for clues, for reasons. But this was frustrating because she could not come up with clear answers.

Some women turn to medical sources for answers to

their questions. They begin to research the condition which caused their child's death—be it their own incompetent cervix or the child's spina bifida. Cathie, for example, became obsessed with trying to find out why the amnion had ruptured, causing her son's malformation. Was it related to the fire that had burned their house to the ground almost six months before? Had she done too much after the fire? She started with the medical library at the hospital and then went on to the public library. The librarians there helped her contact major medical centers to find out more information. She wanted to know!

Kim, too, was filled with questions. Was there anything they could have done differently to prevent her son's premature birth? In the brief time before he died, the doctors encouraged her to spend as much time holding and loving him as she desired. In spite of that, however, in the weeks that followed, she wondered if she should have given up that time with him and had him taken to the intensive care nursery. As she thought of questions, she would write them down, leaving space for answers. If she couldn't find an answer in a couple of days, she wrote a letter to her doctor asking him for answers. He responded with letters that carefully answered her questions.

For two months Kim read everything she could find, asked questions of many people, and searched for answers. It was agonizing and painful questioning, but in the end she felt like her questions were answered. She learned she couldn't have done anything to change the outcome.

Many times the questions surrounding pregnancy loss do not have definitive answers. Persons who miscarry once or twice are told it has to happen three times before extensive tests are done. Trying to find answers to unanswerable questions is frustrating. But the process of formulating questions and seeking answers gives your rational mind something to do while you are attempting to come to terms with your loss. The search for facts and the research activity can begin to give you a sense of having some control at a time when an event totally outside your control has hurt you.

Even when "answers" are found and problems are matched with a reason, there is sometimes little comfort. You may know in your head that there was nothing you did to cause this event. But your heart will still ache—and you may feel that the "real" reason behind your loss continues to elude you. It takes time to accept the fact that there probably isn't a reason.

## JOURNAL

How have you looked for answers and explanations for your pregnancy loss? Did you find yourself thinking in images (like Judy's rescue boat) that somehow seemed to "explain" the event? Describe your image, your explanation.

Did you look for facts, for reasons? Did you ask lots of questions? Did you look for books or articles to help you? Did you get the kind of help you needed for your search? Was your quest for answers respected and taken seriously, or did you find yourself thwarted? How did you feel about the process?

In the end, were you satisfied with the answers you found? How did you feel about the explanations and answers you had?

# 10. COMFORT

Comfort. I longed to wrap it around me like a familiar quilt. I wanted its cocoon to cushion me from the pain. Comfort came in fleeting moments—a warm hug, shared tears, caring words, a prayer. Each was a balm that temporarily soothed my pain. I soon discovered, however, that comfort didn't linger. My wounded heart continued to ache.

I recalled how God's love and comfort embraced me during the tumultuous hours of my hospital stay. While Patrick was away making arrangements for our boys, I felt an overwhelming desire to read the Bible. I had memorized scriptures since I was a child, but I wanted to read long passages for comfort and to help pass the time. After I'd asked several times for a Bible, a nurse finally found one in the fathers' waiting room. I reached for it eagerly. Just holding its solid cover in my hands gave me comfort.

"OK, Lord, now that I have it, where do you want me to read?" I waited expectantly.

His answer came immediately to my mind: *Psalm 40.* The words wove comfort through my heart, and I continued to read the following psalms. Psalms 42 and 43 especially offered solace with a thought that was repeated more than once. "Why art thou cast down, O my soul? and why art thou disquieted within me? hope in God: for I shall yet praise him, who is the health of my countenance, and my God" (Ps. 43:5, KJV). I paused and reflected on the words.

"Now where, Lord?"

*"Matthew 5."*

It wasn't until I reached the familiar passage that it dawned on me that it was the beatitudes. I had known them since I was a little girl. Even so, the verse in the upper corner of the page caught me off guard. "Blessed are they that mourn: for they shall be comforted" (Matt. 5:4, KJV).

Tears welled up in my eyes. "You know I'm going to need that, don't you, Lord," I whispered aloud. I read it again and the words etched themselves on my heart forever.

I cried out to God when I was waiting in the X-ray department. As I lay there studying the dots on the white ceiling tiles, sorrow squeezed my heart even tighter, and I cried out in silent protest. "But, Lord, this is your *special* baby!"

Deep within my innermost being I heard his tender response. "Yes, this is *my* special baby." The emphasis on the word *my* was distinct. I didn't understand, but I knew God was with me. Everyone around me was a stranger, yet I knew I wasn't forsaken or alone.

My mom was another source of comfort when she came to visit the day after I returned home from the hospital. She brought comfort to each of us. In practical ways she showed her love and caring by preparing meals, doing laundry, helping to get the boys off to school and preschool, but most of all by just listening to me. She cried with me and shared my pain.

Sorrow was no stranger to my mom. My older brother's twin sister had died in a house fire many years earlier at the age of sixteen months. Growing up, and especially after I had children of my own, I wondered how Mom and Dad had survived that tragedy.

As we talked, Mom related some of her feelings after Patty's death. "I kept wishing it were a year later," she told me. "I kept telling myself that I would feel better in a year." I wished the same. If only I knew of some way to inject time rapidly into my life so I could be farther away from my pain.

Mom quoted a verse from Psalms that had helped and comforted her after Patty's death. "As for God, his way is perfect; the word of the Lord is flawless. He is a shield for all who take refuge in him" (Ps. 18:30, NIV). I grasped one phrase and clung to it, "As for God, his way is perfect." In the midst of my confusion, it gave me a sense of hope and peace.

One other insight Mom shared with me lodged itself in my mind. "Years ago," she told me, "I made a choice. I decided that even though I don't understand why something has happened, I choose to trust God."

I could identify with that. I was floundering in the waters of not understanding. I definitely did not understand why our baby had died. Looking at Mom's serene countenance, I pondered her words and gleaned comfort and strength from them. How I appreciated her gentle caring. Her tears and hugs and listening bathed me with comfort and love.

Weeks later I wondered where comfort had gone. Pain resided in its place. Would I hurt like this forever? Please, no. The jagged edges of my broken heart pleaded for relief and wholeness once again. Still struggling to believe that our baby had really died, I didn't know the way to wholeness, nor that the journey was going to be so long and hard. I just knew I wanted to feel better.

## REFLECTION

During and after the experience of losing her baby, Judy was aware of God's comforting presence. He spoke to her through his Word in the Psalms and in the prophetic words from Matthew 5: "Blessed are they that mourn, for they shall be comforted" (v. 4, KJV).

Other women, too, have experienced God's comfort and presence in the midst of their loss. Karen lost her baby on Ash Wednesday, the day that commences a seven-week period of meditation on the suffering and death of Christ. Her husband writes the following words about her experience:

> As Karen looked out the hospital window that evening, it was as if God made a cloud formation just for her; there it was—a perfect lamb. She was comforted in knowing that Jesus also suffered and died. The scripture in her devotional book that day was Psalm 91:11, "He will give his angels charge over you to guard you in all your ways."

Joanne also experienced God's comfort after her four-hour-old son died:

> The whole time after Ethan was born and then died, we really sensed God's presence and support. After Ethan had been born, Scott called our pastor and told him what had happened. He also told him that just a couple of days after we had initially found out about the birth defect, I was walking around my kitchen one night, thinking about our upcoming loss. The thought came to me, "God knew ahead of time that His son was going to die." So I *knew* He understood my pain and grief.

Alone in the hospital after her loss, Landie also felt the comfort of God's love:

> All I wanted to do was sleep and block out all this gray, fuzzy happening. And try to pull from the recesses of my mind the comfort of God I knew was mine, if I could somehow make it truly mine and not just words.
>
> I remember saying, "Father, it's Landie. I need you."
>
> I could hear him say, "Landie, come, child, come. Let me hold you, put my arms around you. Put your head on my breast."
>
> As I sat on his lap, the pain started to ease; the hurt, like a lump in my throat that choked me and that I couldn't swallow away, began to subside. The confusion became

sorted and some of the questions I asked that could not be answered, no longer needed answers.

Peace became real. My mind became stable, my insides calm. And I slept—nestled in the love of my Father, God.

Comfort can come in other, more tangible ways, too. It comes through people—relatives and friends—who provide listening ears, open arms, and encouragement for the future. There are people like Judy's mom, who have also known sorrow, but who can say, "There is hope." Kim discovered that other women who had suffered the same sort of loss shared her sorrow and gave her hope for the future.

Comfort can come through other children in the family. They, too, grieve, but they want most of all for their mom and dad to feel better. One dad wrote, "As if an angel prompted Naomi in what to say, she comforted us often in our sorrow with the words, 'I very much love you.'"

This same family found comfort in nature. They lived close to the Pacific Ocean and made frequent trips to the beach. The waters of the Pacific—vast, mysterious, beyond our understanding—reminded them of God who is bigger than our questions and greater than our understanding.

To experience God's presence and comfort, Judy and the women we have just read about and their families had to look for it. They turned to God because, from their past experiences, they believed that he would be there for them. They also allowed others to bring them God's presence and comfort in real and tangible ways.

Experiencing God's comfort in the first days of the loss did not spare these women from also experiencing the pain of their loss. Rather, it was as if Christ entered into their pain with them as they struggled to find their way in the weeks and months ahead.

Sometimes that early experience of God's comfort seemed a long way off. But even so it was a very real part of their experience. For even though they did not understand all the "whys" of their loss, they chose to believe in the God who loved and comforted them.

### JOURNAL

In the time of your loss and in the days after, did you experience God's presence and comfort? Who was involved in bringing this comfort to you? How were you comforted?

If you didn't feel comfort or God's presence, how did you feel? Were you lonely, afraid, angry? How would you like to be comforted, knowing that being comforted doesn't mean that the pain is taken away?

# 11. FEELING SO LOVED

We had just recently moved to Lompoc, but it was not our first time to live there. We had lived in Lompoc as newly-weds, and we had enjoyed renewing old friendships when we returned. Those friends, and others we had only recently met, responded to our loss and were very supportive. Women from our church provided the evening meal for us for several days after the baby died. Others sent cards, letters, and plants to express their concern and love for us. A few people came by the house, and others called on the phone.

Although many people did not know what to say to us, they found their own unique ways of showing us they cared. One woman brought a pie over, even though she hadn't been asked to prepare a meal. Another woman from church, whom I barely knew, called and asked if she could come see me. She came with a bottle of perfume and a card, and just sat and talked with me. I was touched because I knew it was an uncomfortable thing for her to do, particularly since she didn't know me well. Neighbors down the street, whose son played with Kyle, left cookies at the house one day to let us know they cared.

Friends and relatives living out of town also responded

to our loss. My two sisters called from Iowa and Oregon the first evening I was home. My brother called a few days later. My conversations with them comforted me. I felt free to really talk to them and I retold each of them the whole event. That was helpful to me because I needed to talk about what had happened. Each time I shared our story, it became more real to me.

We received many meaningful cards and letters. I skimmed the printed messages and hurried on to the notes that had been personally written. A friend in Pasadena wrote me that her heart ached for days after hearing about our loss. It meant so much that her heart ached for us, that she cared enough to hurt with us.

The couples' group we had been a part of in our Pasadena church sent us a check to buy something for our new yard in memory of the baby. Rita, another close friend from Pasadena, sent me a feminine nightie a few weeks after the baby died. That special gift lifted my spirits and helped me to feel pretty again. It meant a lot to know that she cared and that she was thinking of me even weeks after our loss.

That was what I needed more than anything—expressions that let me know that people cared. I really appreciated hugs. And the concerned look in someone's eyes that said they really cared. Any gesture that conveyed warmth. Simple statements said in love were the most helpful. "I'm so sorry." "I love you." "I'm praying for you." Each one added a rung to our ladder of support and caring.


## REFLECTION

After experiencing a great loss you feel shaken and insecure. Expressions of love and sympathy from friends, co-workers, and acquaintances can be meaningful and helpful.

Judy deeply appreciated all the gestures of love and concern shown to her and her family. Others also tell of cherished expressions of love received in the midst of the pain of losing a child. Paul, the father of a stillborn son, writes:

> Some days after our loss, Karen and I agreed we had never felt so loved. The many prayers, notes, cards, calls, visits, flowers, gifts, and food told us people were thinking of us. It did not make much difference what was said, if anything at all. Some just hugged us and cried. Others shared a testimony of similar suffering, a scripture, a word of support. We found meaning in it all, and never felt intruded upon. Whatever was done or said telegraphed the message, "We care about you."
>
> Karen had heard that when her brother first received the news he had cried with his wife. When he called to see how we were doing, Karen said, "Thanks for crying." He had entered into our sorrow and Karen was comforted by his empathy. Many others said or wrote, "We grieve with you in your great loss."

Kim writes about the importance of their friends' presence at a home memorial service for their prematurely born son.

> We were surrounded by people we loved and with whom we felt at ease. They cried as hard as we did. I could only sit and listen. I could not pray; I did not want to pray. I was exhausted mentally, physically, and spiritually. The people we asked to be with us could pray. They didn't understand "why" any better than we did, but they could pray. We let them. This was the beginning of healing because we didn't have to be anyone but ourselves.

Loving friends and relatives allow you to grieve and be who you are without expectations of how you "should" be acting. Their presence and support helps validate the fact that this loss is significant—a loss worthy of mourning.

## JOURNAL

Did you receive love, support, and sympathy at the time of your loss? Who offered the most meaningful support to you? How did the people around you make their love feel real to you?

## 12. WHY DON'T PEOPLE UNDERSTAND?

I had never dealt with such personal sorrow before. I didn't know that the journey was long and hard. Many of my friends and loved ones had never experienced a loss such as this and didn't know how to respond in a helpful way.

Many people told me, "I heard you were doing so well." Initially, it made me feel good that others thought I was handling my loss well. But as time went on, and the reality of my loss began to penetrate my numbness, I found I wasn't doing well at all. Yet I tried to continue to "do well," to maintain my composure, to smile through the whole experience. I wanted to be the "good Christian" that I thought the people in my church expected me to be. So I repressed many of my true feelings instead of expressing them. When people said things I didn't agree with, I didn't tell them. I smiled, even though at times I wanted to punch them in the nose!

One of the comments that irritated me the most was, "Just be thankful that you have two healthy boys at home." I *was* thankful and grateful that I had them, but they did not take the place of the baby we lost. That baby was a completely different child, and even though we had not known that baby, that child was still loved, anticipated, and wanted. Our boys did not make up for our loss, but some of the people around me did not seem to understand that. And I didn't know how to tell them, for fear of offending them.

I was bombarded with statements such as "God knows best." Or, "It was a blessing." And a lot of Romans 8:28, "And we know that in all things God works for the good of those who love him" (NIV). While I knew in my head the promise of that verse, my heart was too wounded to hear it at that time. Rather than helping me, such comments and scriptures tended to make me angry. Yet, I did not want to be angry, because I didn't think that was a very Christian response. So I buried my angry feelings and pasted on a smile.

Most of the things people said to me were an attempt to make me feel better. What I didn't know at the time was that I could not feel better soon. I needed time to grieve. I sensed that people were uncomfortable with my grief. They were used to my being happy and cheerful. When they saw me feeling sad and depressed, they didn't know how to respond. So they tried to make me feel better. The message I got was, "Start feeling better, and please, the sooner the better." I desperately tried to cooperate.

I had an unquenchable need to talk about what had happened. But with most people, we ended up talking about everything else. The subject of the baby hung silently between us. People were hesitant to ask me questions, and unless they initiated questions, I didn't feel they were comfortable talking about it. I was afraid that I couldn't honestly share my feelings about our loss. I wondered if they could handle my anger and questioning. It was safer to tiptoe around the topic of our baby. Even our pastor, when he came to see us a few days after I got home from the hospital, didn't bring up what had happened. We talked about everything else but the baby. A part of me wanted him to say, "How are you doing?" But he didn't.

I was also hurt by people I just didn't hear from. Shortly after losing the baby, I went to church and a friend sitting in front of me turned around and said, "I wanted to call you, but I didn't know what to say."

I mumbled something like, "That's all right." But my thoughts were completely different. "So that's why you didn't call. I wondered why. I thought it was because you didn't care. You wouldn't have had to say much. Just, 'I'm sorry.' 'I love you.' 'I'm praying for you.' A card or hug could have said those things, too."

## REFLECTION

While Judy received much love and care, she also clearly remembers times when she did not feel loved and cared for. The words spoken, the expressions on faces indicated to her that she should not be grieving, or at least not taking it so hard. These incidents burned themselves into her memory and added to her pain.

When a couple experiences pregnancy loss, few of their friends will have had firsthand experience with grief of any kind. They do not know how necessary it is for you to grieve and may be intensely uncomfortable with your sadness. To relieve their discomfort, they may do or say things to try to cheer you up, thinking that if they can make you feel better, then life can return to normal, and they'll feel better, too. Unfortunately, they do not realize that attempts to cheer you up leave you feeling misunderstood and uncared for.

It is not unusual to respond to such attempts with anger —and then worry that you've destroyed a friendship. Or you may swallow your true feelings, smile, and add the anger and hurt to your grief.

You may feel, as Judy did, that you are expected to quickly put this grief behind you and get on with life. It may seem that your friends are minimizing your loss—and they very well could be. For in pregnancy loss, no one but the mother (and in varying degrees the father and other children) actually experienced and knew that child. No one else is missing that child the way you are. After the miscarriage of their first child, Daureen wrote:

No one knows how to grieve with parents who've lost a child to miscarriage. There's no funeral, no memorial service, no recognition that a real person—someone you love so much—has ceased to be. What a lonely time it was for us. Grieving *alone* is so much harder than grieving *with*.

Some women return to work only to find that their loss is ignored. Either because it is not "professional" to talk about personal matters or because co-workers are embarrassed and do not know what to say, sometimes nothing is said or done. When that happens, it is only normal to feel that no one cares or that your loss is not important.

Often people do not bring up your loss because they are afraid that you do not want to talk about it or that you will be upset by talking about it. They often do not know that you need and want to talk about it—if they are willing to listen.

Kim discovered that she could put people at ease by introducing the subject herself. She found that if she did the telling, rather than waiting to be asked, she could do it when she was emotionally ready and not be caught off guard. She also did not try to say she was "fine" when she wasn't. Looking back, she says she was "factual, not tactful," but feels that her honest sharing of her feelings hastened her healing.

After a pregnancy loss, you need friends who will validate your grief and allow you the time to work it through. Unfortunately, you do not always receive from your friends what you need. Even Christian friends will let you down—either by not giving you adequate time to grieve or by attempting to provide glib answers straight from the mouth of God. Daureen wrote:

What I hated most were the careless comments of well-meaning Christians: "Well, it must not be the right time." Or, "All things work together for good . . ." Or, "It just wasn't meant to be." No one will ever convince me that

God *intended* the loss of my child. What I needed more than anything was someone who would hurt with me, be angry with me—someone who would let me grieve.

It is hard when it seems that your friends don't understand how you feel or that they won't accept how you feel. But even if all of your friends are supportive and helpful, and know exactly what to say and do, they cannot take your pain away. Grieving is lonely, hard work that you have to do for yourself. No one else can do it for you. And sometimes that is hard to bear.

## JOURNAL

What responses to your loss made you feel uncared for or unloved? Which ones made you angry? How did you respond? How do you feel about your response?

Do you sense expectations from others to get over this quickly? To not be so upset? To be more upset? How do you feel about others' expectations of you?

# 13. THE WORLD DOESN'T STOP

Mom stayed with us for a week. How I hated telling her good-bye. As her plane lifted into the sky, my emotions took a nosedive. How was I going to cope without her help?

When Patrick and I left the airport, we had just enough time to pick up the cremated remains of the baby before the funeral home closed. I waited in the car and tried to brace myself while Patrick went in to get our child's remains. I wasn't sure what to expect or what kind of container would be used. But nothing prepared me for the small cardboard box wrapped in white butcher paper and sealed with brown tape. On the top was a piece of paper with the typed words, "Baby Morrow," followed by an eight-digit number.

Everything within me rebelled. How could this be the child I had carried? The impersonal label repulsed me— our child's uniqueness had been reduced to a small box with a number. How dare they? I shed indignant and sorrowful tears.

We began our drive home through Santa Barbara's rush hour traffic. It was a warm day and car windows were down. When we stopped at a red light, I tried not to cry because so many people were close by. Radios blared; people waited at bus stops. Suddenly the bustle of everyday life was intensely annoying. I was amazed by the seeming normalcy of everyone else's life.

Envy flooded over me. I wanted to scream at them in anger, "How can you be so happy? How can your lives be so normal? Don't you know? I had a baby and my baby died. *I'm* dying inside right now."

If I resented the fact that strangers could be happy when I was in so much pain, I was even more resentful of people I knew. Their lives so quickly returned to normal after the initial shock of our loss. Sometimes it seemed that they hardly remembered, they were so busy living their own happy lives.

I wanted desperately for my life to regain its normalcy. I worked hard to get things back to normal as quickly as I could. Yet my steps no longer matched the pace of the world around me. I could not seem to regain my sense of equilibrium. I felt displaced.

## REFLECTION

While immersed in the tragedy of your loss, you may be insulated for a time from the outside world. All your thoughts and energy go toward accepting and making sense of your loss.

It may be almost incomprehensible to you that the whole world has not stopped to take note of your tragedy. How can people go on with their lives when yours has been so unalterably changed? Betsy commented that when she walked out of the hospital after just having been told that the baby she still carried in her womb was dead, she was "surprised to see the world outside was still the same—life went on without us."

As you struggle with your grief, you may be angry, as Judy was, that life does go on for others. Even those close to you are soon busy with their jobs, children, church activities, and recreational pursuits. Their lives seem to be moving faster and faster, while yours has come almost to a halt.

During grief, time seems to change. One hour seems like two. One day drags by like three. It seems to take forever to get through a week. And while your friends may be complaining about not having enough time or that life is moving too quickly, you may long to speed time up. You resent your friends' busy lives and don't like the feeling of having your life suspended. Somehow time seems out of kilter. And as your friends lead their busy lives, it seems that they have forgotten about your loss.

## JOURNAL

Did time seem to slow down or almost stop after your loss? How did that feel?

Did you have a moment in time when it seemed that the world was moving on without you? How did you feel? What did you do or say?

# PART THREE

---

# THE
# STRUGGLING
# TIME

# 14. GUILTY!
# IT MUST BE MY FAULT

A nagging sense of guilt edged the garment of my grief. Somehow I must have been at fault for this to have happened. Most people have normal children. Since I didn't, I concluded there must be something wrong with me. I felt guilty for having an evidently incompetent body that produced such an abnormal child. Concrete clues eluded me as to why this pregnancy failed—instead I was left with uncertainty. Whatever the reason for the failure, I felt responsible for my baby's death, and guilt agreed with me.

Guilt crept into my thinking in other ways. I found myself often remembering a day in the seventh month of the pregnancy when Kyle, six, and Travis, three, had been particularly trying. When I tucked them into their bunkbeds that night, my irritation exploded into anger. But the minute I left their room and shut the door behind me, I was overcome with remorse for my hastily spoken words.

I remember leaning against the wall in the hallway and crying, "Lord, *why* are you giving us another child? I can't handle the two I already have." My words were laced with anger and tears. At that moment I questioned God's wisdom and my capability to be a good mother to three children.

After the baby died, that scene paraded across my mind for months. Had God reconsidered and decided that I could

not handle more than two children? Was I too impatient
a mother to be given another child? Guilt answered with a
resounding "Yes!"

## REFLECTION

After experiencing pregnancy loss, your mind is apt to be
full of thoughts which begin, "If only . . ." "If only I had
called the doctor earlier." "If only I had eaten better, rested
more, taken better care of myself." "If only we hadn't had
intercourse the day before." If only, if only . . .

It is almost impossible not to feel guilt after losing a baby
because there is such a strong sense of having let yourself,
your husband, and your baby down. For whatever reason,
you did not do what you expected yourself to do—produce
a healthy baby. And you are likely to feel guilty, even if you
did nothing wrong.

Guilt feelings may be particularly intense when the pregnancy was unplanned. Margie had always planned on having children, but found herself with mixed feelings when
she discovered she was pregnant sooner than she had
planned to be. She explains:

> Tom and I had been married for less than a year when I
> unexpectedly found myself pregnant. I did not feel ready.
> I didn't think I had been eating all that well and one of my
> first thoughts was that the baby might be born retarded or
> deformed. I remember vaguely hoping that I would mis-
> carry to avoid the risk of such a thing happening.
>
> About ten weeks into the pregnancy I had some light
> bleeding. I called the doctor and was set up to come in that
> afternoon. I wasn't feeling particularly bad, but wondered
> what was happening.
>
> I remember waiting for my exam for a long time. I was
> anxious to get the facts. I don't know how the doctor broke
> it to me, but during the exam, he said that I had passed the

fetus sometime in all the bleeding. He suggested that a
"D and C" be done.

There were tears and I remember the warmth of the
nurse's hand. Were my tears over the loss or over my sense
of guilt for wanting to terminate the whole thing and realizing it had happened?

A part of me felt guilty and ashamed because I had let
Tom down. He was excited at the prospect of parenthood.
Looking back, I think I experienced more guilt than grief.

You are also apt to feel particularly guilty if there were
actions in your past which you regret and consider wrong.
Arlene, who had three miscarriages as well as two healthy
daughters, writes about her past:

> Losing a baby through miscarriage is so very difficult—
> the grief, the guilt. Did I do something wrong? Or maybe I
> should have done this or that. You have all those feelings
> and more when you have had an abortion.
>
> I was nineteen at the time and had been brutally raped.
> I asked myself over and over again as I lay there on the
> stretcher getting ready to have the abortion, "Is it right?" I
> had control, unlike in a miscarriage, but somehow I felt
> like I didn't have control.
>
> It's something I will never forget. I have questioned
> whether or not I did the right thing. At times I felt that
> with the miscarriages, God was punishing me for the
> way I was leading my life and the fact that I had had an
> abortion.

"If only I hadn't had an abortion"; "if only I hadn't wished
I weren't pregnant"; "if only I had been more patient with
the children"—regrets about the past that can't now be
changed. But in the wake of pregnancy loss, these actions
and thoughts come back to haunt you, and you wonder, *Is
this why I lost my baby?*

And in an effort to find a reason, to understand why, it
is very easy to take on the blame and to carry guilt for the

loss. It is easy to decide that it's your fault that the pregnancy failed.

Part of the work of grief is coming to terms with yourself and your past actions. You may be in the habit of blaming yourself for a lot of things, and the loss of this baby is the latest addition to a long string of events for which you feel responsible. Sometimes it is difficult to let go of the guilt because it feels like you are letting go of the one "reason" that you've found for your loss. But you cannot carry the guilt and blame for this loss for the rest of your life and be a healthy person. Eventually you need to make peace with your past and recognize that the loss of this baby was not your fault.

Letting go of the guilt and forgiving ourselves for the past is not easy. But neither is it impossible. You may find it helpful to talk through your feelings and your guilt with a trusted friend. It is often helpful to have someone with whom you can share your feelings of inadequacy and guilt. This person needs to be someone who will not belittle your feelings or tell you that you're being silly. Over a period of time, such a friend can help you face your feelings of disappointment and guilt, help you begin the process of forgiving yourself, and help you see that nothing you did or didn't do was the cause of your baby's death.

Based on her personal experience, Arlene speaks to the value of a listening ear:

> Someone who has not gone through the pain of losing a child or having an abortion cannot possibly understand how you feel. But even when they don't understand, a hug, a reassurance that you still matter to them, does wonders. They couldn't take the pain away, but it helped to have them listen when I got to the point that I could verbalize how I felt. I expressed all my anger, my guilt, and my total frustration with the situation.
>
> Something like pregnancy loss doesn't heal itself easily, but through prayer and identifying your deepest feelings

and getting them out, you can begin to put the experience behind you.


## JOURNAL

Have you found yourself feeling guilty about your pregnancy and its loss? What actions or thoughts have predominated? Do you feel more guilty as time goes on, or less? Is there a friend who can help you with your feelings of guilt?

# 15. THIS IS NOT FAIR!

My pregnancy was a shared event with a few especially close friends. Rita was one of those friends. I stopped by her house to borrow a suitcase just before leaving on a trip, and I couldn't resist sharing my suspicions that I was pregnant. Her face lit up and her words tumbled out that she, too, thought she was pregnant. We were thrilled for each other.

We had great fun as our pregnancies progressed. Rita's due date was just five days before mine, and we compared notes on weight gain and discussed choices for babies' names. We shopped for maternity clothes together. Since I had two boys and Rita had a son, we dreamed out loud of daughters and what fun it would be to dress a little girl in the dainty clothing displayed in the stores. We loved and enjoyed our boys so much and we were so accustomed to them, we could hardly imagine what it would be like to have a girl. We both agreed, however, that above all, we just wanted a healthy baby.

As time went on, Rita and I cringed together as we heard of problems occurring in the pregnancies of other women we knew. A friend of mine had a miscarriage and was devastated because she really wanted a second child. A mutual friend had to have an emergency C-section; it was a close call, with the cord entangled around the baby's neck.

Rita and I became increasingly nervous as we heard things that were going wrong in other pregnancies. A friend told us about her cousin whose third child was a Down's syndrome baby. It was especially upsetting since she had two healthy children and had had no idea anything was amiss. With the knowledge of each new incident, fear gripped us. Finally Rita told me, "Judy, if you hear anything else about pregnancies going wrong, don't tell me. I don't want to hear. I can't handle it."

Even though we had moved from Pasadena to Lompoc in my sixth month of pregnancy, Rita was one of the first persons I knew I should call when I got home from the hospital. Knowing that her baby was not due for another month and that it would be upsetting for her to hear about our baby's death, I hesitated at first to call her. But I knew she would end up hearing from someone else if I didn't tell her.

I put off calling her for three days and then called on Friday evening. She had just left for a weekend women's retreat, and her husband was also away. I left a message with the babysitter to tell Rita's husband what had happened and to ask him to tell Rita when she got home.

She called me after hearing the news; her voice echoed my pain. I appreciated her concern, and we had a good talk. She was thankful she hadn't known before the retreat, as my sad news would have spoiled the weekend for her. I, too, was glad I had waited to call.

A few weeks later, a mutual friend called early one Sunday morning to tell me that Rita had delivered a baby girl. My heart leaped and then plummeted. A girl—her dream came true. I rejoiced for her and yet wept for me. Her joy intensified my sorrow. I struggled to understand. She had her beautiful baby girl and I did not. Why? The angry questions raged within. Why did she get a girl and I did not? Why was her baby healthy and mine was not?

As I sat in church that morning, my tears flowed. Inwardly the questions and confusion continued to bombard my thinking. Rita and I had both wanted a healthy child.

We both wanted girls. She got exactly what she wanted and I got—nothing! Was she more deserving than I was?

I seethed at the injustice of it all but was not able to admit it to anyone else. This inner outburst of rage frightened me. I wanted to be in control. So I carefully gathered up my unanswered questions and anger, put them in a box labeled "Do Not Open," and buried it deep within my heart.

## REFLECTION

When Judy heard the news about Rita's baby girl, she felt that she should feel glad. What she actually felt was intense envy and anger. Why had Rita gotten a healthy baby girl and she had gotten nothing? It wasn't fair!

But Judy had a hard time facing up to her feelings. They were powerful, and they frightened her. If she really allowed herself to feel them, to give them free rein, what would happen? She didn't know, but she was sure she didn't want to find out. So she bottled up her anger and her envy and put them away.

Judy grew up in a home where anger was denied and for the most part unexpressed. It was not OK to be angry. Angry feelings were looked down upon as unchristian. Because of this, she had had very little experience in dealing with the kind of intense anger that she felt at the loss of her baby. She didn't know that anger is a normal response to being hurt, and losing that child was a hurtful, painful experience.

Judy was also afraid of her anger because it didn't fit her perception of herself. She was a nice, pleasant person, not an angry, out-of-control one. She didn't want to be angry. She didn't want to be out of control. She didn't want to alienate her friends and family. So she didn't express her anger, but inwardly she seethed.

Judy is not the only woman to have difficulty with anger after suffering pregnancy loss. Joanne's fourth child only lived for a very short time after birth because of anencephaly. Shortly after her loss, her college roommate came for a visit with her five-week-old son. This child weighed 7 pounds 12 ounces at birth, exactly what Joanne's dead son, Ethan, had weighed. Joanne writes:

> I sat and watched her nurse, bathe, and care for her first child, while it ripped me up inside. When we went out to eat or went shopping, people would ask her how old the baby was, how many children did she have, and comment about how cute he was.
> I found my heart screaming out, "I had one too!" What pain! My friend just wanted to be near me, to show her support and love. But her good intentions didn't help me. I was ready for her to leave.

In the next few weeks Joanne found herself experiencing conflict in one relationship after another. She had a falling-out with her father, she and her best friend were no longer so close, and misunderstandings clouded another significant friendship. In the midst of all this her husband, who was in the military, was transferred and they were moving. She writes:

> I was an absolute witch. *I was so angry.* I treated my family horribly. At one point I tried to leave Scott and the kids. I thought it would just be better if I weren't around. I couldn't see that I was doing anyone in my family any good.

Joanne experienced the anger she felt, but it was troubling because she found herself reacting so negatively to people who were trying to help. And she was ashamed of her anger and the way she treated her family. She felt like a failure and a bad person because she was so angry.

Anger is powerful and can be destructive. Sometimes it is most destructive when you try too hard not to be angry. Then when you least expect it, something happens, and you fly off the handle with the power of the anger you were trying so hard to suppress.

Some fortunate women have been able to acknowledge and express their anger throughout their experience and have found that it was helpful and healthy. Kim, for example, writes:

> I did not expect myself to be happy or good. I expected to be mad and angry. I was mad, angry, frustrated, and hurt! I felt like a piece of paper someone crumpled up, stomped on, and then slammed against the wall in anger. I felt that way twenty-four hours a day for over two weeks. At three weeks I felt less crumpled, less angry, less tense. By two months I felt mad and angry when I wasn't concentrating on something else. By six months I felt angry only when I couldn't control the situation. Then I responded in anger at any irritation—not just in response to the death of our son.

From the beginning, Kim gave herself permission to be angry. And the people around her also gave her that permission. They let her know that it was normal to be angry, and they didn't expect her to put on a smile and continue as though nothing had happened. Because Kim felt free to express her anger, she escaped the destructive repercussions that so often accompany repressed anger. Even so, she found herself responding in anger to what would have otherwise been minor irritations.

As Kim indicated, anger is an emotion that you feel for a considerable period of time after your loss, although its intensity and duration will diminish over time. It will be helpful if you can find one or two people with whom you can freely share your angry feelings—people who will listen and validate your loss and let you feel that it is appropriate to be angry. Finding someone to whom you can express such anger might help keep you from expressing it in inappropriate and destructive ways.

Other outlets for feelings of anger are exercise and writing. A good brisk walk, playing tennis, or jogging provide a way for the energy of anger to be released. Writing out your angry feelings in your journal can also provide a feeling of release. Paper is a safe place for the feelings of anger and envy that are a normal part of loss. And no one gets hurt when feelings are written for no one's eyes but yours. Somehow, once expressed on paper, the feelings of anger are less powerful and less frightening.

Judy hoped she could get through the experience of losing her child without facing her anger. She learned later that experiencing and feeling her anger was a necessary part of the work of grieving her loss.

## JOURNAL

What aspect of your loss seemed most unfair to you? Did you respond to the unfairness of this loss with anger? How did you express it? If you didn't express it verbally, what did you do?

How do you feel about being angry? Is it easy or hard for you to be angry?

What makes you most angry about your loss? What situations make you feel angry? Is your anger damaging your relationships with friends, your children, or your spouse? How have you chosen to deal with your anger?

# 16. GOOD DAYS, BAD DAYS

I teeter-tottered between good days and bad days. On good days I woke up feeling in control and "on top of things." I breezed through the day with a smile; I played with the kids and handled my daily tasks. Optimism prevailed. I sometimes felt a twinge of guilt for feeling so good. On those days I was convinced that all bad days were behind me. I told myself, "I'm OK now. I'm over this. I won't be crying about it again. It's all in the past. I'll be fine from now on."

The bad days bowled me over with newfound sorrow. My emotions did a complete flip-flop. I dressed in depression and dragged through the day. I cried at the slightest provocation. Seeing babies or pregnant women triggered crying spells. So would TV advertisements flaunting babies and baby things. The tiny baby clothes in department stores, pink and blue "welcome, baby" cards on the racks, babies in infant seats in the grocery carts—all made my heart wince with pain.

One bad day stands out in my memory. It was a day when I went to K-Mart and discovered that a photographer was there taking baby photos. I steered away from the cooing babies posing for pictures, yet in every aisle I found either a pregnant woman or a tiny little baby. And it seemed every baby was a girl, dressed in a pink frilly outfit.

My composure unraveled. I quickly finished shopping and retreated to the car. I drove home blinking back the tears. The pain was suffocating. When I walked into the house, Patrick took one look at my face and exclaimed, "What's wrong?" I burst into tears, and between sobs I told him about seeing all the babies. He immediately drew me into his arms.

Another sunny October day about a month after my loss also stands out vividly. Letters came from two friends, and I opened them eagerly, as I hadn't heard from either one since the baby's death.

One letter began with, "I was really sorry to hear about what happened," but then continued with several pages of joy and excitement about *her* new baby. She and I had been pregnant at the same time, she with her first child. She had shared with me her misgivings about being a mother. Now with the birth of her son, her doubts were dispelled—her son was wonderful, and she loved mother-hood. Her letter was typical of a new mother, and I knew she didn't mean any harm, but it tore me apart to read about the cute things her baby was doing when I had no baby to write back about.

The other letter was from a friend who took several pages to tell me how excited she was to be pregnant for the second time. At the very end of the letter she mentioned that they were sorry to hear about our loss.

I cried off and on and felt extremely depressed the rest of the day. All day I tried to shake the depression hanging over me. I re-read the letters again and again, searching for sympathy and understanding. I found none. I only saw their joy. I was happy for them, yet it was so very painful for me.

In spite of the fact that I had so many times experienced dramatic shifts in my emotions, I was never prepared. Each time sorrow sneaked up on me, I staggered from the new blow. I was angered by my inability to be consistently in control. I upbraided myself, "I'm supposed to be over this by now. What's wrong with me anyway?" Each time, I was determined it would not happen again. I vowed to be in better control of my moods and feelings.


## REFLECTION

Going through grief is a little bit like being on a roller-coaster blindfolded. You have no control over the car's movements—one moment you're up, the next you're down —and because of the blindfold, you are never prepared for what comes next.

One day you wake up smiling. The sun is shining. You make a list and finish the tasks on it by the end of the day. You go to bed feeling good and thinking that you are through with feeling sad. Life is good again.

The next day you are overwhelmed with sadness. Nothing goes right; you can't seem to finish the simplest task. You wonder why you bothered to get out of bed. How can you feel so sad when yesterday you felt so good? Are you always going to feel this depressed? Is life always going to be this up-and-down, this unpredictable?

Judy's bad days were often triggered by seeing pregnant women and/or babies or by receiving letters from friends full of news of pregnancy and newborns. With each of these experiences, she was confronted with the reality of her loss and her own sadness about that loss. What happened to Judy is not unusual; many women who experience pregnancy loss have times when they are overwhelmed by sadness and other times when they feel their grief is behind them. Six months after her child was stillborn, one woman wrote:

On good days, I'm at peace, content with my life and the memory of my daughter Jennifer. On bad days, I just want to die. When friends, even when strangers, have babies, it's bad. I feel somehow that I've lost my place, been sent back to the starting line while everyone races past me. On those days I do anything to avoid facing the awful fact of my loss: I had a little girl; she died.[1]

Each bad day is an opportunity to confront and again experience your loss. This is not something that you really want to do. But it is a necessary part of your journey through grief.

The good days are like beacons of hope along the way to let you know that not all of life is sadness and grief. You will be able to smile and laugh and feel like your old self once again.

On the bad days, it is difficult to believe that you'll ever feel good again. On good days you want desperately to believe that your sadness is over. Part of getting through grief is learning to expect both good and bad days and to accept them as they come.

Eventually the roller-coaster ride will be over and your blindfold will be removed. Good, or at least ordinary, days will increase; bad days will be fewer and fewer. There will be fewer peaks and valleys. But in the meantime, it seems that you're on a ride that will never end.

## JOURNAL

Have you experienced the good-day/bad-day roller-coaster ride? Describe your feelings and actions on a good day. Describe your feelings and actions on a bad day. How do you feel about not being able to control the ups and downs of your emotions?

---

[1]Donna Moriarty, "The Right to Mourn," *Ms.*, November 1982, p. 84. Used by permission of the author.

# 17. OTHERS GRIEVED, TOO

When Mom was still with us, I was somewhat startled when she shared how she was grieving over the loss of her grandchild. Her words locked around my shoulders and shook me momentarily out of my own pain. I felt stupid that I had not realized that this was a loss for her and Dad, too. She mourned for us, yes, but she also knew her own grief in this loss. Her sorrow whispered caring to my bruised heart.

I was more aware of Patrick's mourning for our child. I recalled his tears at my bedside in the hospital and knew his grief ran deep. I also knew that the most significant chapters in his life were the most difficult for him to talk about. So even though his words were few, I knew that he, too, was hurting.

However, I was so engulfed in my own sorrow, I was also almost oblivious to the grieving of my children. The day after our baby's death, Kyle raised his hand several times in his first-grade class. Each time his teacher acknowledged him, his offering was the same: "My mommy's baby died."

This incident was relayed to me a few weeks later by a woman in our church whose daughter worked as an aide in Kyle's room. I was surprised and touched. After his initial outburst of grief, I had overlooked Kyle's sorrow. It hadn't occurred to me that he, too, needed to talk about it.

Weeks later I had one of my bad days. I had been fighting back the tears and sadness all day. Still feeling out of sorts in the evening, I tried to settle the boys into bed. Their typical bedtime antics annoyed me, and my unhappiness grew as they ignored my admonitions. Finally, I yelled at them in frustration and immediately regretted it.

I apologized to them for my inappropriate anger. I explained to them that I was having a bad day because I missed our baby. Immediately Kyle responded, "I miss our baby, too."

"Me, too," piped Travis from the bottom bunk. Their expressions of sadness surprised me. As far as I was aware, they barely even remembered that we had had a baby who died. We exchanged tender hugs and kisses, and I left the room comforted by their caring.

## REFLECTION

Because you are the one who carried the baby in your body, and then experienced the pain of not completing the pregnancy as you expected, you may feel very alone in your grief. It was to a large degree your loss.

But the members of your family—your husband, your children, your parents—also suffered a loss and also grieve. So do your close friends.

But while you're struggling with your own feelings, which often seem to change from minute to minute, it is difficult to even notice or comprehend the grief of those around you. That others grieve over your loss may take you by surprise, as it did Judy when her mom and then her children expressed their own grief to her.

While it may seem that young children can't comprehend a pregnancy loss, they are very aware of the emotions of the people around them. They know when there is something wrong. And if they are not given explanations, they will very likely assume that whatever the problem is, it must be their fault!

Judy discovered that sharing her sadness with her two boys allowed them to speak of their own sense of loss. While it's difficult to be in tune with your children when you are grieving, sharing your feelings of loss and sadness with your children will give them the opportunity to share theirs. It will also give them the opportunity to comfort you. And it will reassure them that you still love them and are not angry or sad because of something they did.

Husbands grieve, too. But your husband may express his grief very differently than you do. It may seem to you that he gets over it very quickly. Many times the basic ways husbands and wives have of dealing with problems of any sort are very different: one of you may be very rational, the other more emotional; one of you may be very action-oriented, the other may want to take much time and thought before making decisions. In normal circumstances you are able to tolerate your differences and even laugh at them. But when your styles differ in grief, you may be tempted to think that your spouse is not really grieving—just because he's not doing it the way you do.

And as much as you may have shared the pregnancy, it was you who carried the baby. And that makes a difference in the way you grieve. One woman who miscarried wrote:

> My husband and I had made a point of sharing this pregnancy as much as possible. We told people, "We're pregnant" and "Jorge and I (or Mary and I) are going to have a baby." Yet, I miscarried; "Mary lost the baby." Suddenly, we weren't together in this; I was ultimately responsible for the death of our child.

About six weeks later she wrote,

> Today I read an article stating that typically the father is a trimester behind the mother in experiencing the pregnancy.

This is a great comfort to me because Jorge seemed to recover so quickly. While my grief and pessimism continue, he
gets frustrated with me. He's ready to move on, to look
ahead, and I feel hurt that he can so easily forget. It helps me
to realize why Jorge's grief is so different from mine.[1]

Parents and inlaws experience the loss of a grandchild,
too. Their grief is real and genuine. Joanne commented that
her mom really missed being able to hold Joanne's son, who
died shortly after birth. He was the only grandchild that she
didn't get to hold. Another woman wrote:

My parents were incredibly helpful and supportive. They
were very saddened by the loss. "I didn't realize how much I
was looking forward to the baby," my mother said. She and
my father, who is a family doctor, searched for information
for me, and the things they sent were very helpful. One of
the articles they sent pointed out that the depth of grieving
for a fetal loss is irrespective of gestational age. That fact
stuck in my mind and was a great weapon against the many
future comments that diminished what I was going through.[2]

Even close friends experience the loss of your child. They
were looking forward to their own relationship with that
child. Now that is lost. Betsy wrote about Sandy, her friend
and pastor's wife, who often let her know she still thought
of James and missed him, too. This acknowledgment helped
Betsy feel less lonely in her grief, as she was tempted to
think that no one else missed her son and that she was all
alone in her grief.

Acknowledging the grief of others while you are struggling with your own may seem difficult, if not impossible. It
may seem that no one—not your husband, your parents,

---

[1] © February 1986, "Miscarriage: Remnants of a Life," by Mary Davis. Reprinted
with permission from *Marriage and Family Living* magazine (pp. 15–16), Abbey
Press. Saint Meinrad Arch Abbey, Saint Meinrad, IN 47577.

[2] Marian McDonald, "Miscarriage: The Silent Wail," *Birth Stories: The Experience
Remembered,* ed. Janet Isaacs Ashford (Trumansburg, NY: The Crossing Press,
1984), p. 145. Used by permission of the author.

your children—can possibly understand how you feel. And to some degree that is true. But if you can hear their grief, you will probably feel less alone with yours. And while their expression and working out of their grief may be done differently than yours, it is comforting to know that others, too, are grieving because of this loss.

## JOURNAL

Who else is grieving the loss of this child? How have they expressed their grief to you? Was it comforting to you to know they were also grieving? Have you felt that some weren't grieving enough? How has this made you feel?

# 18. LIFE IS BACK TO NORMAL?

For my six-week postpartum appointment, I went back to my doctor instead of the doctor who delivered the baby. I hadn't seen Dr. Arlen since the morning he had sent me to have the ultrasound test; however, he had called me while I was in the hospital and expressed his shock and caring.

He was kind and sympathetic during my appointment. He asked me if I had seen the baby. I told him I'd caught a glimpse of the baby's face and how thankful I was for that. Relief spread over his face. He explained that women who don't see their babies tend to envision "phantom babies" because they so desperately want to know what their child looked like. After having carried and loved the child, it's vitally important to see that child. Not seeing the baby at all is far worse than seeing a baby with abnormalities. Otherwise, it's harder to deal with the grief later.

After he told me that, I was more grateful than ever that I had at least had that glimpse of the baby's perfect little face. It was etched forever on my mind.

Travis was at a friend's house so I had some free time after my appointment, and I wandered around the nearby community of Solvang. Going to Solvang was always a treat for me. I enjoyed the quaint Danish architecture, the bakeries, and gift shops.

Today, however, was different. Depression hovered over me as I went from shop to shop. My feet dragged. The merchandise bored me. My joy at having time to shop dissipated. I determinedly trudged from shop to shop, trying to shake off my growing depression. I finally gave up and drove the twenty miles home.

On the way home my tears flowed. I reviewed the appointment in my mind. How similar it was to my other postpartum appointments—similar, yet so drastically different. This time there was no newborn to examine, weigh—and, yes, admire.

Our picture wouldn't be added to the doctor's wall of photos of proud parents with their newborn babies. How I had enjoyed looking at that colorful wall during my OB appointments. Joy radiated from each smile and punctuated the many thank-you notes posted beside the pictures. It was painfully obvious that there was no place for my sad face and my collection of sympathy cards.

By the time I arrived home, my heart was weighted down with sadness. A deep sigh escaped as I pulled up in the driveway, and I wondered if the sadness would ever end.

## REFLECTION

After a pregnancy, the six-week post-delivery checkup marks the return to a semi-normal life. Usually your body and your energy levels are getting close to pre-pregnancy "normal," and there is a growing, healthy six-week-old infant to admire.

A postpartum checkup without a baby is another step into the reality of grief. There was indeed a pregnancy; there was indeed a baby. But now you're no longer pregnant and there is no baby.

The six-week checkup is a time and place when many women seek answers to the unanswered questions about their loss. Some doctors do well with this, some do not.

Your doctor may feel like he failed, even if nothing he did or didn't do had anything to do with your loss. Because of his feelings of failure, he may react defensively to your questions.

Many women feel very let down when their doctors never acknowledge the loss of their pregnancy. Cathie's baby was delivered by the doctor on call, who was not her regular OB physician. She expected to hear from her regular OB doctor, to at least have him say, "I'm sorry this happened." He didn't contact her, and she went to see the doctor who delivered her baby for her post-delivery checkup. She commented, "He wasn't much comfort, but at least he seemed to care."

Leaving the post-pregnancy checkup, you are forced to face the fact that your life is not going the way you thought it would. At this point in time, you expected to either be more and more pregnant, or to be caring for a new baby. As you leave the doctor's office, the reality of the loss hits once again. You are not pregnant; there is no baby. No wonder your feet drag.

## JOURNAL

What was your post-pregnancy checkup like? Did your doctor acknowledge your loss? Was he sympathetic or unsympathetic? Were your questions answered to your satisfaction? How did you feel when you left the office?

# 19. I SHOULDN'T FEEL SO SAD

Sadness permeated my days. I missed our baby. How I wanted that child. I often retraced the past year in my mind.

This pregnancy hadn't just "happened" but had been given much thought. Patrick and I had always planned on only having two children, but as our sons got older, I found myself wanting one more. Patrick assured me that he would be happy either way—it was up to me.

But it was difficult for me to know what was best. I thought about it constantly. The list of pros and cons ran through my head continually. To have a child three years after Travis meant I had to decide soon. (Almost exactly three years separated Kyle and Travis and I liked that spacing.) Yet I couldn't make up my mind. Indecision reigned.

Finally one sunny day in December of 1978, these same tiresome thoughts deepened the well-worn ruts they had often traveled. I was making the bed at the time, and as I pulled up the heavy white bedspread, I suddenly exclaimed aloud, "I'm *tired* of this! Lord, if you want us to have another baby, then let me be pregnant by next June. If I'm not, then we'll know we're not supposed to have any more."

I was startled and amazed by my own words. It was as if I listened to them after I spoke. I marveled as a tremendous weight unexpectedly lifted. I felt released from my obsessive thoughts. I was able to get on with my life.

When, a couple of months later, I suspected that I was pregnant, I immediately remembered my conversation with God. (Patrick and I had continued to use our effective birth control, and it had never failed to work before.) When my pregnancy was confirmed, I was elated—and certain that this baby was God's special baby for us. I was convinced that this baby wasn't our idea, but his.

I enjoyed to the hilt the pregnancy with this special baby. I spent hours thinking about what kind of child this would be—what special personality it would have, what God's plan for it was, whether it was a boy or a girl. While I would really have liked a girl, my primary wish was just for another child to round out our family.

I had other dreams, too. I was looking forward to having a child in the cooler weather of fall and to being able to bundle up this baby without worrying about heat rash, as I had with my August babies. The baby's due date was October 13, and I was hoping for a birth on October 8, my mom's birthday.

Most of all, I was anticipating the joy of having a two-month-old at Christmas time. Christmas was my favorite time of year, and I enjoyed thinking of how special it would be to celebrate Jesus' birth with an infant in my arms.

With our baby's death, all my plans and dreams were dashed. There wasn't a baby born near Mom's birthday. I wouldn't hold a baby in an adorable Christmas outfit. The baby who was so "special," who was to make our family complete, didn't live.

Yet in spite of all these losses, after the first week or two I didn't feel like I should still be grieving. "After all," I told myself, "I never knew this baby." My loss was not nearly as great as others I knew about or even had heard about on the news.

When I heard of three children in one family dying in a fire, my heart ached for the parents. How could they stand pain like that? I told myself sternly that I shouldn't feel so sad when others had losses much more horrendous than mine. In fact, it seemed that anyone's loss was more profound than mine.

I would recite in my mind all the reasons I shouldn't feel so sad. I had two healthy boys, a terrific husband, we were back in Lompoc . . . the list went on and on. Yet sadness continued to be my unwelcome companion. I was troubled by its constant presence and felt guilty for feeling sad. Soon my guilt and sadness ran together.

## REFLECTION

Losing an expected baby is a loss—a big loss. But in many ways, it is a loss consisting of many smaller losses. For example, the size of your family and the spacing between children will be different because of this loss. You may have been anticipating having an infant at a special time of year, such as Christmas or Easter, or a child born on or near someone's birthday. Or perhaps this baby was that first son or daughter—maybe even a first grandchild. Now that special child is not going to be an ongoing part of your family.

These losses may seem insignificant in and of themselves. But they *are* losses, and it is normal and appropriate to grieve over them. And taken together, they demonstrate how much your plans and expectations have been drastically changed.

Very early in the pregnancy you probably began to dream dreams for that child. Someday he would go to school, learn to read, bring friends home for basketball in the driveway. Someday she would learn to roller skate, go out on that first date, learn to drive. A whole life lay ahead.

With the failure of your pregnancy, the fantasies and dreams you had for that child are now shattered. The pleasures and joys of parenting you foresaw for yourself have to be given up. And it's not easy to let go of hopes and dreams. Betsy, whose son was stillborn, wrote:

> Losing one that you've waited so long for is so hard. James was my dream child, the one I've longed for since our marriage began. The child of my dreams—a boy. . . . He was the child I dreamed Jim and I could conceive. The son that Jim would love so dearly. I guess James will always be the child of our dreams.

Yet in spite of all the small losses and your lost dreams, you may find yourself trying to minimize your loss with words such as, "It was only a baby that I didn't even know." Or, "I was only twelve weeks pregnant. I shouldn't be so upset."

Even in early pregnancy, the child can be very real to you. An article in one medical journal says:

> Recent research . . . has shown that attachment of the mother, and to some extent the father, to the infant begins to develop as soon as fetal movement is felt. Indeed, the attachment may begin even earlier among some couples, especially if the pregnancy has been long awaited or difficult to achieve. Thus, even if the child never lived within the home environment, or even independent of the mother, it is important . . . to realize that the parents' sense of loss can be significant.[1]

When the pregnancy failed, you lost a child—and that is something worthy of sadness.

Judy eventually learned that trying to talk herself out of her grief by counting her blessings didn't work. Neither did minimizing her loss by comparing it to the seemingly greater losses of others. She eventually came to realize that she had lost a special, longed-for child. Her loss merited sadness and so does yours.

[1]Olle Jane Z. Sahler, M.D., and Stanford B. Friedman, M.D., "The Dying Child," *Pediatrics in Review, III* (November 5, 1981): p. 162.

## JOURNAL

Have you thought of the many small losses that were involved when your pregnancy failed? List as many as you can think of. As you look at your list, add a word that describes your feelings about each loss you've identified.

What were your plans and dreams for this child? How long had you been dreaming about this child? How do you feel realizing that you have to give up those dreams?

Are you allowing yourself to be sad? Have you tried to talk yourself out of your sadness? Look at the losses you listed above and at your lost hope and dreams. Are these losses worthy of sadness?

# 20. WHERE ARE THE LISTENERS?

Even weeks after the event, I found myself really needing to talk about what had happened. I needed to relive the experience. I needed to share the details with other people as I tried to come to grips with it.

Initially, I was allowed to do that with my loved ones and friends. Then Mom returned to Oregon and busy schedules reclaimed the lives of those around me. Yet, more than ever, I needed to talk about it.

I talked with Patrick, and he was sweet and understanding. It wasn't long, however, before our differences emerged. With his quiet and introspective nature, Patrick dealt with his grief on his own. Being much more verbal and expressive, my feelings demanded an outward release. I sensed, too, that Patrick felt I should be moving along more quickly and not needing to talk about it as much as I did. So I sought someone besides him to listen to me and help me work through my feelings.

When I tried to broach the subject with the two women who were my closest friends, I felt a wall go up. My words bounced off it and landed back at my feet like a half-inflated basketball. At first I thought it was my imagination, and I tried again. Still no response—just uncomfortable silence, often followed by an obvious effort on

their part to change the subject. It hurt. I didn't understand. After having been with them, I would come home
feeling depressed and sad.

The need to talk increased. I yearned for understanding
listeners. No platitudes, no pats on the back, no glossing
over the pain. Just someone to listen with empathy and
understanding.

But my two best friends could not do that for me. Their
inability to listen compounded my grief. I felt like they
were, in many unspoken ways, telling me it was time for me
to move on, to leave this grief behind.

As I was still fairly new in the community, I didn't know
where else to turn for listeners. I began to feel that no one
cared about my grief. And since my friends didn't help me
sort out all the painful emotions I was experiencing, I
thought I had no choice but to bottle up my emotions. So
I resolved to quit talking about my loss and to get on with
life in the best way I could.

What I didn't know when I made this resolution was that
I had already met the two women who would ultimately
become my listeners, my "lifesavers." One Sunday evening
in late September about two weeks after my loss, the boys
and I went to McDonald's with a couple from the church,
Tom and Joan (Patrick was at work). They had sent a plant
to our home after the baby's death, and I was touched because I had just met them a few weeks earlier.

When we left McDonald's, they came over to our house
and we talked some more. It wasn't long before the conversation turned to the subject of our baby. They asked questions and listened with genuine interest and concern. How
easy it was to share with them.

On December 10, almost three months after my baby's
death, I attended a baby shower for the first time since my
loss. I chose a seat on the outskirts of the festive group, near
a wall. I found myself seated next to Kathy, a petite red-
haired woman about my age.

She and I had met previously at church when I was still

pregnant. At that time we had discussed my obvious pregnancy, and I had shared with her then the story of this baby's specialness.

As the shower progressed, Kathy and I became more and more involved in conversation. The party faded into the background, and we barely glanced at the gifts as they were passed around. We discussed many subjects, but it wasn't long until the topic was the baby I had lost. She leaned toward me as she listened and her blue eyes and kind expression encouraged me to go on. I felt the pressure inside ease as I was allowed to express my pain and sadness. The evening ended too soon, even though Kathy and I were among the last to leave.

After the holidays I began to spend more time with both Joan and Kathy. Often our three families got together for an impromptu meal. While our husbands talked and our children played, we had our own conversations. Often those conversations were times when I talked and they lovingly listened.

I discovered that I could be real with them. I didn't have to put on a happy face and pretend everything was all right if I was having a bad day. They relived with me the entire labor and delivery, the shock, the sorrow, and the hurt and disappointment of not being understood by those around me.

They never said, "You shouldn't feel that way." They listened. They didn't try to make me feel better with pat phrases. They listened. Their empathy and caring shone in their eyes as I poured out my heart to them. The more they listened, the more my wounded heart was assuaged.

## REFLECTION

Judy knew she needed someone to listen. She has always been a person who likes to talk, one who can turn even small incidents into entertaining stories. Losing her child was a large event in her life, and she needed to talk about it. She needed to talk through the event and her subsequent feelings about it again and again.

She turned to her two closest friends and was shocked and disbelieving when it seemed that they couldn't hear her. She kept trying, but still no results. She couldn't believe it. These women were her friends. What was wrong?

Months later, she realized that those two friends were not the ones who would be able to help her work through her grief. Because of unhealed hurts in their own lives, they could not listen to her sorrow. Listening to her pain unearthed their own buried pain and made them uncomfortable. By responding to her with silence or by changing the subject, they let her know that they did not want to hear any more about her loss. This was devastating to Judy's fragile sense of self-worth.

She needed to talk and she needed friends who would listen—friends who could hear the feelings behind her words and respond with warmth and caring. Friends who could let her know that she mattered to them and that her pain and grief were real and important. Friends who could affirm her worth as a person, even as she struggled with her grief.

She did eventually find such listeners. But it took time, and in the meantime she was lonely with her grief. And, like many other women, Judy found that her husband, although sympathetic, just couldn't be her only outlet. Kim, who lost her baby in the sixth month of pregnancy, also found that her husband didn't want to talk about it as much as she did. So, to bridge the gap between them, she would share with him information that she discovered in the course of her research. But she did most of her talking about her feelings with others, especially her mother-in-law. She says,

> My mother-in-law was extremely supportive. She let me talk and she listened. She talked and I listened. We talked about being sick, being pregnant, having labor, delivering

the baby, *all* my feelings about God, life, kids, husbands—
everything. I think all my talking helped me heal more
quickly.

Joanne, whose son died a few hours after birth, would
call Judy from Ohio and ask her if it was "normal" to feel
the way she was feeling at different times during the first
year after her loss. She knew Judy could accept her feelings and understand because of having been through a
similar experience. Also Joanne found a friend in Ohio
who had lost a child due to Sudden Infant Death Syndrome (SIDS). They were able to share their experiences
and to encourage one another.

Having listeners who can affirm your feelings and give
you hope that you will survive this journey through grief is
important and necessary. Your friends can be a tremendous
help to you in this.

Sometimes, as in Judy's case, your friends are not capable
of being the listeners you need. You may need to make an
effort to discover the people who *can* listen to you without
being judgmental or putting you down. Actually, it's possible you already know them and you're just not aware of it.
People like Kathy and Joan, who by their empathetic listening, affirmed Judy's worth, affirmed her struggle, and gave
her hope that she would get through that difficult time.

If you cannot find listeners who seem to understand, you
may want to consider professional short-term counseling to
help you work through your grief. Counselors are trained to
be empathetic and nonjudgmental. They also have the train-
ing to help you move through your grief, to help you avoid
getting "stuck" in one phase of the experience.

Another option is to join a support group of parents who
have suffered a similar loss. Your doctor, local hospital, or
childbirth educators may know of such groups. In the book
*Birth Stories: The Experience Remembered,* Marian McDonald
says that after her miscarriage, she contacted a pregnancy
and parenting center and was told about a pregnancy loss

support group. For her this group was an important part of
the recovery process.

> At our first meeting it was as if someone had physically
> removed a great heavy burden that was bearing down on
> my shoulders. We all shared our feelings about our losses,
> about the wonderful, anticipated beloved babies we had lost
> at the end of our first trimester, at sixteen weeks of preg-
> nancy, at five months, at birth, on the day after birth. We all
> knew we had lost our babies—either babies we knew well,
> whose fingers and toes we had seen and touched and whose
> faces would be forever imprinted on our minds, or babies
> whose future birth we could only dimly imagine. For each of
> us there was a deep and irrevocable loss that had changed
> our lives. Through the group we discovered a collective
> sense of loss and grief that we could slowly transform,
> through sharing. On that first night we experienced great
> waves of feeling, interspersed with long moments of quiet,
> unrestrained weeping. But in time we moved to a place
> where we could be more in control of our feelings, without
> denying them, without being afraid of them. From this kind
> of sharing comes a sense of hope, fragile and sometimes
> elusive, but hope nonetheless.[1]

Even with friends, counselors, and support groups, there
may still be times when you feel that there is no one available to listen. Using your journal to write out your thoughts
and feelings and then reading it back to yourself is a way of
learning to befriend yourself. Women often tend to dis-
count their own needs and feelings as they take care of the
other people in their lives. You may hardly know your own
feelings because you don't take the time to identify them
and listen to them.

Consistently writing about your loss and grief in your
journal is a way of validating the life-changing experience

---

[1]Marian McDonald, "Miscarriage: The Silent Wail," *Birth Stories: The Experience
Remembered,* ed. Janet Isaacs Ashford (Trumansburg, NY: The Crossing Press,
1984), p. 146. Used by permission of the author.

and a way of learning to listen to yourself. You have things to say about this experience; you know it was important and worthy of grief. As you put these thoughts and feelings on paper, you are giving yourself the time and space to sort out all the ramifications of your loss. You learn to listen to yourself and accept yourself. Such self-knowledge and self-acceptance may be an unforeseen benefit of your loss experience.

## JOURNAL

Do you have an empathetic and understanding listener? If so, how do you feel after talking to this friend? If not, how are you trying to fill this need?

Have you felt with some friends that they didn't, or couldn't, listen to you? How did this experience make you feel?

Have you thought about or tried a counselor or a support group? If so, how does this kind of listening experience feel?

Are you learning to listen to and accept yourself?

# 21. BUSY, BUSY

The dishes had been returned from the meals friends had brought us. The thank-you notes were written for the plants and other remembrances. The boxes from our recent move were all unpacked and we were settled in our new home. The time I had reserved for caring for a newborn hung heavily on my hands. I determined to fill it.

I volunteered to help in Kyle's first-grade classroom one morning a week. I started taking a weekly dough-art class. A friend taught me counted cross-stitch. I met with our energetic pastor, and he suggested some projects that I might be interested in tackling.

From among his suggestions, I chose to compile an Advent booklet to help enhance the Christmas season for our entire church family. I threw myself wholeheartedly into the project. Enthusiastic women met for an evening of sharing ideas for crafts, traditions, and recipes. The "small booklet" grew larger than imagined. A few other women pitched in and helped with typing and proofreading. We double-checked recipes. The details were endless.

I welcomed the hectic schedule. Sandwiched between the booklet and other activities were my personal Christmas preparations. My lists were endless—gifts to make, cards to send out with our annual Christmas letter (difficult to write that year), shopping, baking, and wrapping. My mind was teeming with "things to remember," leaving room for little else.

I fell into bed each night exhausted, and sleep came rapidly. I was grateful, for the quiet of bedtime offered too much time to think without interruption. I preferred going to sleep immediately, without a moment to remember that our baby died and how much I missed that child.

Yet in spite of all the flurry of activity, there were moments when I did remember. Interwoven with the Christmas carols was my song of mourning. I was afraid to listen to it or even acknowledge its presence. It was just too painful.

After all, I loved Christmas. This was my favorite season of the year . . . wasn't it? I couldn't admit that my anticipation of Christmas was blemished. A tiny baby wouldn't nestle in my arms in front of the Christmas tree. There would be no ornaments reading "Baby's First Christmas."

"If I think about it, I might fall apart," I'd remind myself fiercely. So I'd shed a few tears and with great resolve shove down my feelings one more time. Throwing myself once again into my frenzied schedule, I desperately tried to put behind me the loss of our child.

## REFLECTION

Judy's life plan included moving to Lompoc, getting Kyle started in first grade, getting the house organized and the nursery ready, and then spending the fall taking care of her new baby. When there was no new baby to care for, she seemed to have more time than she had activities with which to fill it.

Judy was also trying desperately not to feel her anger, her sadness, and her loneliness. Since these painful feelings emerged during unfilled time, she vowed to fill all her time with meaningful activity.

Other women have also used busyness as a way to handle

their grief. Anne found her friends unsympathetic after her miscarriage. Their message to her was: "You weren't pregnant enough to cry and grieve. You're fine, Anne, just stay busy. It's like spilled milk; you clean it up and keep going." So that's what she did. She kept busy—too busy to think. And she buried the pain deep within herself, only to have to deal with it years later.

Cathie, on the other hand, had no choice in her busyness. She was overwhelmed by events totally beyond her control. To begin with, her house had burned a few months before she lost her baby. Then six days after her baby died, her husband, Craig, was rushed to the hospital for a spinal tap. He had been ill with Valley Fever, a severe viral infection, for several months and the doctor discovered that his skin was now involved. After four days in their local hospital, Craig was sent to Stanford, where it was hoped that the doctors could treat him with a new experimental drug. They made the trip to Stanford and came home hoping that with rest and this new drug Craig would recover.

In the meantime, Cathie and Craig were also trying to rebuild their house. Now Craig struggled with having almost no energy as a result of his illness. Cathie says:

> I cried in the shower. The baby's death just wouldn't go away. I grieved in silence as I tried to cope with the rest of my life and tried to provide some semblance of family life for our other son. Only God's grace helped me survive.

Judy, Anne, and Cathie were all too busy to mourn their losses. Judy and Anne were busy by choice; Cathie was busy because of her circumstances. But they all discovered that their busyness blocked their recovery process.

Their intentions were not wrong. Providing meaningful activities for themselves after their losses could have been therapeutic. Ceasing all activity and brooding over their losses would not have been healthy, either. But they all had so much going on that there was no time to reflect on their losses and to mourn the death of their children.

Many women have found that some structured, meaning-ful activities are helpful after their loss. It gives them some-thing else to focus on, as well as an area of their lives over which they can exercise some control again. Some women find this in their jobs. It's a place where they're comfortable and they function well. Betsy wrote: "Going back to work has been good. It's given my days a new focus. I'm glad I have a job."

Each day for several weeks after her miscarriage, Kim planned a short outing of some kind. Often it was only a trip to the store, a garage sale, or a second-hand shop, but it was something to look forward to and something to do. Kim also reports that she baked and burned several dozen cookies in the weeks following her loss. Although she planned activi-ties, Kim did not overwhelm herself with many tasks and new responsibilities. Avoiding the pressure of a tight sched-ule, she came and went when she felt ready. And she contin-ued her grieving.

After a painful loss, it is a temptation to fill your life with activities that make you feel better about yourself—activi-ties that give your life meaning and validity. The pitfall is in becoming so busy that your busyness anesthetizes you to your grief. Judy discovered that busyness held her grief at bay for a time, but it was not the pathway to healing.

## JOURNAL

How would you describe your activity level in the days and weeks following your loss? Do you feel too busy or not busy enough? In reviewing your activities, do you see any pattern of using busyness as a way of avoiding the pain of your loss? Are there any activities you need to drop? Are there activities that affirm you and make you feel good about your life? Are you doing these? Are you giving your-self adequate time to mourn?

# 22. CHRISTMAS JOY?

Christmas. Each year I savored its distinctive joys, from inhaling the pungent scent of evergreens to singing the traditional carols. I didn't expect Christmas to be any different after our baby died. Nothing prepared me for fresh sadness. I tried to shove down the call of mourning that rose up anew. I filled the hollow spot inside me with all my busy preparations and tried not to think about our baby that was missing from the celebration.

As the holiday season progressed, I sensed I was losing control; I struggled to keep the lid on my simmering emotions. I knew if I let down my guard, all the carefully pressed down feelings would come spewing out. I resolved to remain in control and not spoil Christmas.

Once the Advent booklet was finished by early December, I threw myself into our family's Christmas. From morning until night, I prepared gifts and cards and decorations, each project wedged between the daily chores of caring for my family. My frantic activity increased with the daily opening of a window on our Advent calendar.

December 24 arrived but I was not yet ready, and I was crushed with disappointment. Patrick's mom and younger brother, Dennis, arrived from Southern California earlier than I had expected and found the house overrun with unfinished projects. The boys and I were in the middle of our annual spree of making cut-out sugar cookies. Flour and dough, frosting and sprinkles covered the counters and sifted down to the floor. I wanted to plop down in the middle of the kitchen and cry. Instead I swallowed my tears and apologized for the mess.

That afternoon I was in our bedroom when Mom Morrow came in, pointing to her back, not saying a word. Fear strangled me as I realized she couldn't breathe and wanted me to hit her on the back. Knowing Patrick was trained in Heimlich, I ran and got him off the phone.

Dennis and I watched helplessly as Patrick wrapped his arms around his slender mom and again and again did the maneuver. Nothing worked. Her face was turning blue and I envisioned her gone . . . I had never known such fear and panic and hopelessness. I ran to call the paramedics. As I dialed, I heard the shout, "She's OK! She's breathing!" When I hung up the phone, I trembled all over with relief.

We were all terribly shaken. The death of Dad Morrow almost five years earlier was still too fresh in our memories. We were so grateful that Mom was all right, but the episode left us with our nerves rubbed raw.

After we calmed down somewhat, Dennis went with me to pick up a last-minute Christmas gift. A violent wind and rain storm raged. Intersections were flooded, and the car brakes failed several times. Tension tightened its grip as I concentrated on avoiding hitting the cars in front of me.

We arrived home to learn that a log had rolled out of the fireplace, setting off the smoke alarm and jarring Patrick out of a nap. Mom Morrow was working in my tiny, messy kitchen trying to help get on the lovely Christmas Eve meal I had planned, new recipes and all. Everything took longer than I had anticipated, and by the time it was ready, we had to gulp down the meal.

We rushed to ready ourselves for church. Our family had been asked to do the Advent wreath ceremony at the Christmas Eve service that night. As we hurried into church, only fragile threads were keeping me together, and I prayed they would hold. How relieved I was when we got through our parts without botching them. Sitting quietly for the rest of the service momentarily soothed my frayed emotions.

We returned home, and after a quick cup of eggnog, I set to work to finish my Christmas preparations. Most of the presents had not yet been wrapped, and I stayed up until the wee hours while everyone else slept. I fought tears as I wrapped, chastising myself with every piece of tape and each bow. "Judy, you should have been better prepared; what's wrong with you, anyway? You worked all these months, and you're still not ready. You can't do anything right, can you? No matter how hard you try, you fail."

When I awoke Christmas morning, I ached with exhaustion and longed to bury myself deeper into the bedcovers. I had never been so unexcited about Christmas. I did my best to smile and tried to respond to Kyle's and Travis's excitement as they opened their gifts.

Wrapping paper carpeted the living room, but one more gift remained. At his dad's request, Kyle opened the front door—and exploded with joy when he saw a brand new bike waiting for him on the porch. His excitement at getting his first bike brought tears of joy to my eyes. But with those few tears of shared joy, I discovered that buckets more were waiting to be shed. I sucked them in and managed to hold them back once more, all the time hoping and praying my weakening dam wouldn't burst.

Physically and emotionally drained, the tears stayed close all day as I tried to be a good wife, mom, and hostess. Mentally I checked off each task: clean up the mess, prepare Christmas dinner, see off Mom and Dennis. I trudged through the day. I wanted to collapse, but couldn't allow myself to. I had invited several families over for an early evening get-together.

All afternoon I flew around the house, chasing clutter and preparing finger foods. Our pastor and his family came, a couple who had no relatives nearby, some neighbors—the house soon filled with chatter and warmth.

Afterwards I was numb with fatigue, but I couldn't let up yet. The boys and I were leaving on the train for Oregon the next day, and I still needed to do laundry and pack for the three of us. I consoled myself with the thought that after I got to Oregon I could relax and rest. That was hard to even imagine.

## REFLECTION

When the world seems to be full of happy faces, sparkling lights, and glowing candles, you may feel that you and your grief are out of place. Somehow it seems almost cruel to be celebrating the birth of a baby two thousand years ago, when you don't have the baby you were expecting.

Judy tried to bury her feelings of loss and sadness by creating the perfect Christmas for her family. If she kept busy enough, if she made everyone else happy, maybe she too would feel happy. Yet in spite of her best efforts, it wasn't picture-book perfect. Things went wrong. And her feelings of anger and loss almost broke through. But she didn't want to spoil Christmas for everybody else, so she held her feelings back.

In many ways, Judy was still denying the reality of her loss. To really think about her loss was too sad, so she didn't allow herself to do that. But the discrepancy between her true inner feelings and the perfect holiday she was trying to create was almost too great to be borne.

Other women who have experienced pregnancy loss have also found the Christmas season to be difficult to get through without losing control of their emotions. One woman wrote in her journal:

December 10: "What child is this, who, laid to rest, on Mary's lap is sleeping?"

This Advent and Christmas season are painful. I'd planned to be six months pregnant by now and had hoped to experience more fully this special season. Instead, the constant reference to the anticipated birth of Jesus deepens my own emptiness.[1]

When the joy of Christmas seems overwhelming, it might help to remember the first Christmas. True, there was great joy, but it was also a time of difficulty and pain, particularly for Mary. She became pregnant out of wedlock —a shocking, disgraceful event. She made the long, uncomfortable journey to Bethlehem even as her delivery date neared. She gave birth in a stable, hardly the place she would have chosen. Pain and joy were very much intertwined that first Christmas.

And so it is for you, the first Christmas after your loss. You are more aware than ever of what you don't have. The pain is very real. But as you experience your pain, you also open yourself to the possibility of joy, hope, and healing.

## JOURNAL

What was the most painful part of the first Christmas after your pregnancy failed? Did you hear your song of mourning underneath the Christmas carols? Did you try to make Christmas more special than normal, or did you try to ignore the holiday festivities as much as possible? Were there any moments of joy or hope during Christmas?

---

[1]© February 1986, "Miscarriage: Remnants of a Life," by Mary Davis. Reprinted with permission from *Marriage and Family Living* magazine (p. 16), Abbey Press. Saint Meinrad Arch Abbey, Saint Meinrad, IN 47577.

# 23. FEELING LIKE A FAILURE

The boys and I arrived in Salem, Oregon, after a twenty-hour train ride. My sister Nancy and her daughter were visiting from Iowa. Our other sister, Becky, and her husband, Dan, came from Portland. And our brother, Jim, and his wife, Jane, and their son were able to join us for a few days from Eugene.

I enjoyed talking with my family and playing games together. Yet the change of pace was a shock to me. It felt strange to have nothing to do other than care for the boys and help out with meals.

Patrick, the boys, and I had visited Oregon the previous April when I was pregnant. On that trip, Jane, who was expecting her first child, and I had had great fun discussing our pregnancies. We imagined out loud how delightful it would be to have cousins so close together in age. I had shared a similar conversation with Karen, a woman from my parents' church, who was also expecting her first.

The interim months had blossomed with new life. Karen had a boy in June. And Jane's son was born in July. Then in November, Nancy announced she was pregnant with her second child. One afternoon during my Christmas visit, the three gathered in my folks' living room. Conversation and laughter intermingled while the two babies, Matthew and Danny, cooed at each other.

I stood at the entrance to the room, watching their animated faces as they admired the two babies and Nancy anticipated hers. Snatches of their conversation wafted over to me—conversation which in days past I had loved. But as they talked of pregnancies, nursing, feeding schedules, I longed to cry out, "I was pregnant. I had a baby, too." But I didn't get to talk about my baby; I had no baby to share or delight in. I didn't even have a picture. I felt so cheated and left out.

A fresh wave of pain assaulted me, and the dam inside began to give way. I ran to my parents' bedroom and barely got to the door before the flood of tears hit. I stood in the middle of the room and cried and cried. Mom came in and tried to comfort me, but nothing could console me. After months of pushing down feelings and hiding behind busyness, the hurt was begging to be acknowledged. I didn't know what to do with it. I only knew it wasn't going to allow itself to be ignored any longer.

The rest of the week I slept a lot. I hoped to avoid any more outbursts of emotion. One late morning, Nancy and I were standing at the wide mirror in the bathroom putting on our makeup. As we talked together, I kept remembering people in Lompoc I had forgotten to remember at Christmas. I thought out loud: "Oh, I should have gotten something over to the Millers. I should have remembered to take some goodies to the Bartons."

I was continuing my string of laments when Nancy suddenly interrupted me. "Judy, quit saying 'I should have' all the time. Look at all you *have* done!"

I bristled with anger. What right did Nancy have to tell me what I should or shouldn't be saying or feeling? My strong reaction amazed me. Nancy began listing some of the things I had done for other people during the holidays. She said it bothered her that I was so hard on myself.

"Judy," she said, "you did more than three ordinary people at Christmas. How much do you expect of yourself?"

I was chagrined. As far as I was concerned, my self-condemnation was justified. I was a failure—and nothing I did could make up for that.

## REFLECTION

When Judy got to Oregon, all the busyness of her super-woman routine stopped. She no longer had the activities of her daily life to shield her from her pain. Instead, she was confronted with it again and again. New babies of family and friends, a pregnant sister—everywhere there were reminders of her "failure." And that's how she saw it. Others succeeded in having healthy babies; she failed.

Her primary identity in life at that time was as "wife" and "mother." And she felt defective. I remember that during the week we were together she said to me, "I'm not a good baby-maker. Kyle was born with a hole in his heart. And this baby was terribly deformed."

Other women have also shared that sense of failure. Kim wrote,

> I was angry because I had failed to nurture and deliver a full-term, healthy son. I had failed God somehow. I wasn't a good parent. I *wasn't, wasn't, wasn't* any quality you could mention.

Kim and Judy both experienced a deep sense of inadequacy and worthlessness because they had failed to do what they needed to do to fulfill what they saw as one of their major roles in life—mothering.

Even women who have careers and whose identity isn't based entirely on their role as wife and/or mother experience a profound sense of failure when their bodies fail to produce healthy babies. Barbara Berg, a professor of history, had a late-pregnancy miscarriage as well as a baby born dead. She found that her educational attainments and a successful career did not protect her from feelings of inadequacy and failure. She says, "I certainly believed that a woman's ability to bear a child had absolutely nothing to do with her identity or her competence, yet when I went through these things I felt that it did."[1]

When your pregnancy failed, you not only lost a baby, you lost a part of yourself. You lost a part of your "mother" identity, and this is true even if you have other children. You lost a part of the sense of yourself as a competent, capable person. And for a time those losses may overshadow every other good thing in your life.

Judy truly had done more that one Christmas than any three normal people would have or could have done. To some degree, her many projects were an attempt to compensate for her deep sense of worthlessness. She proved over and over again that she could create things of value. Yet because of her overwhelming sense of failure, she could not appreciate what she had done. She gave herself almost no credit. All she could see were the negatives—she hadn't been ready when Patrick's mom and brother arrived, she hadn't remembered all her neighbors and friends "properly." On and on went her list of failures. And her list began and ended with "I'm not a good babymaker."

## JOURNAL

Since your loss, have you found yourself thinking, "I'm a failure" or "I'm no good at anything?" What situations trigger those thoughts? What have you done to combat these feelings of failure? Has it been successful?

[1]"Specialists Helping Women Ease Miscarriage Trauma," *Los Angeles Times*, 4 December 1981.

# PART FOUR

---

# HEALING

# 24.  FACING THE PAIN

I had not thought beyond Christmas and my trip to Oregon. Both had consumed my thoughts and my time. As my vacation days dwindled, I felt like I was treading water—trying to keep the smile from sliding off my face, trying to maintain cheerful conversation, trying to be the happy mom/ sister/daughter. Most of all, I was trying not to think about what was now uppermost in my mind, the death of our baby. My fingers were slipping one by one as I struggled not to lose my grasp on self-control.

Gloom boarded the train with me as Kyle, Travis, and I left Oregon to return home. I looked forward to seeing Patrick, but had no anticipation for anything else. The only thing waiting for me at home was time—unoccupied time that would allow me to think and remember. The prospect of facing all that empty time scared me. *How would I fill it?* I wondered.

That night on the train, I settled the boys down with their blankets and pillows. After reading awhile, I curled up in the reclining seat and was soon lulled to sleep by the rhythmic motions and sounds of the train.

In the middle of the night, I suddenly awoke. I sat up, heart pounding. As I glanced frantically around the coach and out the windows, I suddenly realized the cause of my distress. The words thundered in my mind, "My baby died, my baby died." Without warning, the sorrow I had buried for over three months now erupted with volcanic force. My heart burned with the painful truth as if it had been seared with a branding iron. I caught the scream in my throat and buried my face in my pillow. My tears flowed silently as I fought for control.

As my heart slowed its racing pace, I leaned back in my seat. I could still feel remnants of the burning pain in my heart. Wide awake, I pondered what had just happened. I was stunned and could hardly sort my thoughts. As my shock wore off, overwhelming sadness crept in. I eventually drifted back to sleep wondering what lay ahead.

After we arrived home, the blank calendar taunted me with its unfilled spaces. January had always been at the bottom of my list of favorite months. This year's rating was worse than usual as "the blahs" invaded with greater force than ever before. A fog of depression threatened constantly, and I often succumbed. I couldn't shake the feeling of being out of sorts.

I tried not to think about the baby, but there were so many reminders. Pregnant women and babies abounded; surely there had never been so many around before. The empty nursery, now turned into a den, continued to haunt me. I would be looking for something in our long desk drawer, only to be startled anew by the cardboard box with the baby's remains, tucked in a back corner of the drawer. Just the sight of the box upset me. (Patrick and I had discussed different possibilities of what to do with the remains, yet nothing had seemed right and appropriate.) And the quiet routine of my days was in itself a constant reminder of the baby missing from our home.

One afternoon, depression triumphed, and I moped around the house. Patrick was home, and I unloaded on him some of my feelings and frustrations. I explained how I was trying not to think about the baby because it upset and depressed me so much . . . and how little I was succeeding. He sat down on the bed beside me and put his arm around me. Gently he said, "But, honey, you need to think about it. That's exactly what you should do. That helps you to be able to accept what has happened. That's what I had to do after Dad died."

A small beam of understanding sliced through the grayness. We talked about his dad's death five years earlier and the process of mourning Patrick had gone through. He had done it so quietly and on his own that I hadn't been totally aware of his pain and sorrow. Relief spread through me as he assured me that my thoughts and feelings were normal.

After the conversation with Patrick, it was as if I had been given permission to grieve. Gradually I allowed myself to go back to that sorrowful September. Once more I heard the doctor's words. I walked again through the trauma of the labor and delivery. I relived the silent delivery room, the shock and pain. I faced the hurt of not being understood in my loss. When the sadness overwhelmed me, I shared my journey with Joan and Kathy. Each time they listened with caring. As I thought about and expressed each fragment of pain, I felt better. No longer did I need to suppress my feelings. Layer by layer I uncovered each hurt, and with each revealing, the weight of my grief lightened.

## REFLECTION

When you lost your baby, you didn't lose something that was of no significance to you. You lost a child that you valued and were looking forward to knowing and loving. Having a child may have been the fulfillment of your lifetime dream of motherhood. When that child didn't live, your loss was great and so was the intensity of your grief.

One woman described her feelings after her loss in these words:

I feel as if I'm clinging to my life by the slenderest thread while a tornado whips me around. Now that everything is over, the profundity and finality of our loss sets in with a vengeance. The emotions that come up are staggering—great gales of weeping set off with such innocuous reminders as the time of day the baby was born; alone, screaming rage in my apartment when the grocery store forgets an item in my order. And it seems that the farther I get from the day of her birth, the more she is lost to me. . . .[1]

The strong emotions that come from your loss can be frightening and overwhelming. You may not want to admit you feel them, much less tell anyone else. But grief calls for the authentic expression of the feelings you have. And to express those feelings means you will probably be and feel less in control than usual. It will also mean that sometimes you may act in ways that are contrary to what you think is expected of you.

You may be tempted to be "courageous" and react stoically and unemotionally to your loss. But the pain of grief is inviting you to step into the process of healing by giving yourself the freedom to experience and express your feelings. One author suggests:

Tears and courage need to be seen as close relatives to each other. Courage is to face straight-forwardly the pain and sorrow of loss, and to deal with it; courage is not to suppress it and mask it with a phony facade of fortitude.[2]

Kim's pregnancy came after six years of marriage and after trying for over a year to conceive. She and her husband wanted four children. When her baby was born prematurely at twenty-five weeks, she lost not only the son who had been so wanted, but she also lost assurance that her future would be what she expected.

[1]Donna Moriarty, "The Right to Mourn," *Ms.*, November 1982, p. 82. Used by permission of the author.
[2]William A. Miller, *When Going to Pieces Holds You Together* (Minneapolis: Augsburg, 1976), p. 53.

Although crying is sometimes seen as a sign of weakness, emotional instability, or lack of faith and hope, Kim gave herself the freedom to cry. She says, "I cried and cried, hours each day for the child I had held so little—this tiny being, who needed to be loved, cradled, soothed, and would never know these things." She reports that her crying periods occurred with lessening frequency during the first six months after her loss, depending on the reminders that came up. Kim didn't run from the pain of her loss and she seemed to know that crying is a therapeutic expression of emotional pain.

Judy spent most of the fall running from the pain of her loss. She knew it was there, yet she avoided facing it for as long as possible. Part of her reluctance to experience her pain was her perception of herself as someone who was "doing well" in handling this crisis. After not doing so well in producing a healthy baby, at least she was "doing well" in facing her tragedy. She didn't want to give up that identity.

And so she ran from the pain. She filled her life with activity and more activity. She went to Oregon to visit family. But after all her work and the visit, empty time loomed ahead. And her pain rushed in to fill the void.

The pain that erupted from her inner being with such intensity and force in the dark on the train was a delayed grief reaction. The pain that she could have been feeling bit by bit all fall, but had systematically resisted and run from, ambushed her.

In the dreary January days that followed, she continued to try to ignore the pain. But since she was no longer so busy, she found it impossible to do. And Patrick encouraged her to face it—to remember her baby and to mourn her loss.

In the months ahead, as she talked with Joan and Kathy, and as she experienced the reality of her loss, Judy began to experience some healing. When she faced the pain and walked with it instead of running away from it, she actually began to feel better.

## JOURNAL

Has it been difficult or easy for you to face the pain of your loss? Have you found yourself running from it as Judy did? Did the intensity of your feelings frighten you? Have you experienced being "ambushed" by suppressed pain? Have you found ways to express the pain and sorrow you've felt? Write about your relationship with your pain.

# 25. "GOD, I'M SO ANGRY!"

One night in late January I watched a movie on TV while I folded mountains of laundry. The kids were tucked in bed for the night, and Patrick was at work. The movie was based on the true story of a young woman who had cancer. As the story progressed, I became more and more involved. The laundry was soon forgotten as I was swept up by the story. Tears streamed down my face when the movie concluded with the young woman's death.

I cried for the woman and her family, but I soon realized that my tears were more than those normally shed over a sad movie. I continued to cry as I thought of Wanda, a friend whose father had recently murdered her mother. I cried for all the pain and sorrow and sadness in the world. And I cried for me.

I had cried before with great feeling and depth, but this time was different. These tears weren't just of sorrow; they were also hot tears of anger. The anger I had so carefully boxed up after the birth of my friend Rita's baby could no longer be repressed. I could no longer pretend that everything was fine and that I wasn't angry. I cried harder, dampening the mounds of laundry around me.

When my tears let up momentarily, I felt driven to write what I was feeling. I grabbed a pen and some notebook paper and without hesitation began to write. My hand couldn't move fast enough as I poured out the sorrow and anger boiling inside me. My handwriting even *looked* angry.

Anger surged anew each time I had to refer to our baby as "it." I furiously scrawled page after page of the blue-lined paper, even mentioning the tiny clothes we had waiting that had never embraced our baby. I listed several friends who had recently had healthy babies. I named others who were pregnant. I lashed out with my "whys." My tears continued to flow as I wrote.

Finally, several pages later, I stopped. I felt drained, but better. Peacefulness seeped in where anger had spilled out. What a solace it was to admit my anger. It cracked open the door for healing to enter and begin its work. I was amazed that I felt closer to God after spewing out my anger than I had during the months of holding it in and trying to ignore it. I sensed that he was right there with me, not holding my anger against me, but wanting to help me work through it. I felt foolish that I hadn't realized earlier that his response would be one of caring and comfort, even in the face of my anger.

Somehow over the years I had gotten the false notion that Christians didn't get angry—that anger was wrong and unspiritual. I realized later that that very premise was what kept me from expressing my anger much sooner, along with wanting to demonstrate to onlookers how well I was doing. Experiencing God's understanding of my anger gave me a new perception of God—I was freed to be totally honest with him. At last, I knew that God could handle my anger and would love me just the same.

## REFLECTION

When Kim lost her son, one of her friends said to her, "Kim, you know, you might be angry at God, and that's OK."

Kim said, "I'm not just angry with God, I'm furious with him!" She goes on to say:

I yelled at God. I asked him "Why?!!!" I demanded answers now. I screamed and yelled silently and out loud for six to eight weeks.

Unlike Kim, Judy carried her burden of anger for months. She was angry at a world where tragic, sad things happen daily. She was angry at a world where young mothers die of cancer and where babies die before they are born. While it was difficult for her to direct her anger toward God, in the end she realized that her anger included God himself. He could prevent these needless tragedies—why didn't he?

It was foreign to Judy's personality and theology to wrestle with God, to throw her questions and her anger at him. Yet, after months of trying to accept her plight and getting nowhere, she finally let out her questions and anger. And when she did, she began to experience peace and God's love for her. He no longer seemed so far away.

Judy didn't realize that when she wrote out her anger and threw her questions at God, she stood in a very biblical tradition. In the Bible—particularly in the Psalms, the prophets, and in Job—we see people who questioned God, complained, challenged, and protested. And we don't sense that they were far from God, but rather just the opposite. They were close enough to trust him with all of their feelings, not just the ones that they deemed acceptable.

And their angry, questioning, complaining words became their prayers, the means by which they connected with God. And instead of distancing them from God, the words brought them closer. In wrestling with God, they ended up experiencing his embrace.

Daureen experienced God's embrace when she took her questions about the miscarriage of her first pregnancy to him. She writes:

In moments of intense pain and anguish, I remember imagining myself beating the chest of my heavenly Father, while he held me with his hands. Somehow I knew he was holding me tight, but I was so angry, so confused, so hurt . . . all I could do was hit him helplessly, asking, "Why? Why?" He never let go.

Daureen, Kim, and Judy didn't receive immediate answers to their questions. But in the voicing of their questions, their hurt, their anger, they discovered that God was there with them and that he cared.

## JOURNAL

Have you felt angry at God because of your loss? Have you been able to express your anger to him? How have you done this? How did it feel?

If you find expressing anger with God difficult to do, read through the Psalms. Notice how often the Psalmist expresses his anger, his hurt. When you feel ready, write a psalm to God, expressing your anger and your hurt.

# 26. ANOTHER CHILD?

Within a few weeks of our baby's birth and death, I found myself longing for another child. The desire surprised me. The conversation with my doctor in the hospital was still fresh in my memory. After telling us the results of the ultrasound test, Dr. Corlett discussed with Patrick and me the possibility of having another child. He advised us it would be wise to have genetic testing done before we made a decision.

I responded vehemently. "We will not be having another child. This one wasn't planned, and we won't be having another one." I was adamant. I couldn't imagine setting myself up for so much pain and disappointment again.

Still my desire for another baby increased as the weeks passed. I struggled with my feelings. Common sense told me we should have genetic testing done before making a decision. Emotionally, I didn't feel I could handle that process. Then I'd remind myself of the baby's severe abnormalities and that Kyle was born with a hole in his heart. Although Kyle's heart didn't require surgery, the fact remained that two of our three children were born with defects. How could I consider having another one? My unfounded but real guilt pressed me toward genetic counseling. Yet the thought of all the procedures, testing, and paperwork repulsed me. Patrick didn't find it appealing either. I was also afraid the results would tell us no, and I knew I couldn't handle that harsh finality. We wrestled with the dilemma and came to no conclusions. Six months passed.

A month later I was pregnant. I was shocked I had conceived on the twenty-fifth day of my menstrual cycle, the only time we didn't use birth control. I greeted the knowledge of my pregnancy with mixed emotions; nervous joy bubbled within me. I was relieved the decision had been taken out of our hands.

I was "up-front" with God. "You must know what you are doing because I don't think I could handle that again." I knew, however, it *could* happen again and knew of others who had lost more than one child. I tried not to dwell on that possibility but prayed and hoped for a healthy child.

I chose a doctor closer to where I lived for this pregnancy. He, too, was caring and understood my anxieties stemming from my recent loss. He advised me at my first appointment to have an amniocentesis done in Los Angeles when I was four months pregnant. I agreed to it, knowing that no matter what the test indicated, it would at least give me time to prepare myself mentally and emotionally. Waiting three weeks to hear the results was difficult. Time dragged and my imagination played, filling my mind with "what ifs."

It was July 28, my birthday. I was home alone putting on my makeup when the phone call came from the lab in Los Angeles. I held my breath as the woman's voice read me the test results. "Everything came back normal." Joy tingled through me, followed by sheer gratitude. What a terrific birthday present!

She went on to ask me if I wanted to know the sex of the child. Patrick and I had agreed that we would like to know, so I answered yes.

"It's a boy." A small wave of disappointment rippled through me, since we had hoped for a girl. But I was elated at how little it bothered me. The baby was healthy! What cause for joy! Patrick, the boys, and I rejoiced together after I told them the good news.

There were others who missed the point of the celebration, who bemoaned the fact that it was another boy. It angered me that they concentrated on the insignificant. Why couldn't they instead focus on the important fact that the child I was carrying was normal and healthy? I realized they simply didn't understand.

Even with the knowledge of the positive test results, I still had moments of apprehension. Flashbacks to the quiet delivery room momentarily chilled my anticipation. My imagination created scenes of something going wrong with the baby, and fear would return. I prayed often and peace replaced the fear, but it was an ongoing process.

I tried not to dwell on negative possibilities but focused my thoughts and love on the active baby within me. His boisterous activity comforted me and filled me with hope. He was much more active than the last baby. He literally bounced at times, especially during "forte" choir numbers. It was easy to smile as I sang, since his movements often tickled me. I delighted in carrying him.


## REFLECTION

Immediately following the loss of your child, whether it was in early or late pregnancy, you probably had strong feelings about whether or not you would try to have another child. Many people feel as Judy did, that they definitely do not want another one. Yet, as time goes on, much to their surprise their feelings change. Because of this, it is important not to make permanent decisions which will prevent you from having more children until you've had a few months to live with your decision.

Joanne went ahead with her planned tubal ligation after her fourth pregnancy, even though her son didn't live. At that point she didn't want to take the 5 percent chance of having another baby with anencephaly. She couldn't imagine going through the loss of another child. So even though some good friends questioned her about her decision, she had her tubes tied the day after Ethan's birth and death.

Just days later her husband commented that he still had wanted to have four kids. Joanne's heart went thud. At the time Scott had felt it was mostly her decision, but soon they were both regretting having acted so quickly. Joanne looked into the possibility of having a reversal but decided against it. She wishes that she had not made the decision to be permanently sterilized until she was through grieving. Although she enjoys the three children she has, she would have liked to have the option of making the decision about a fourth child in a more rational state of mind.

Carol, on the other hand, gave herself more time to make a decision about having another child. She had a five-year-old daughter when she and her husband decided they would like to have a second child. A few months later the doctor told her she was pregnant. They were thrilled. But their excitement was short-lived when the doctor decided he'd made a mistake—she wasn't pregnant after all. But in a few months Carol did become pregnant and shared the news with all her friends. Then when she was twelve weeks pregnant, she miscarried.

After time passed she reassessed her situation. She looked at her age (she was thirty-six) and the pain of her two disappointments. She decided that she couldn't put herself in the position of having to go through that grief again. She and her husband decided to look into adoption, and almost two years after her miscarriage, they adopted three-year-old Jon.

Cathie's experience was different from either Joanne's or Carol's. After she lost her baby, Cathie was, in her words, "obsessed" with getting pregnant again. Her life plan was to have her children close together, and losing her son messed up her plan. She became very frustrated when she had difficulty conceiving, and it was over a year after her son's death before she became pregnant. But because of her previous loss, she was apprehensive about the pregnancy.

Cathie's apprehension is shared by other women who have experienced the failure of pregnancy. One woman wrote after her miscarriage:

> Often my deepest hurt stems from being robbed of the joy of hearing that I'm pregnant. I'll never hear those words again with the same naive joy, that same innocence of spirit. I know that in future pregnancies, there will be a cloud over the news and I'll wonder, "Is it going to happen again?"[1]

A few weeks later this woman did become pregnant again, and she wrote, "I'm frightened and cautious and fearful of feeling too close to this child."[2]

It is a risk to love another unborn child when you have known the pain of losing a child. Daureen lost her first baby in a miscarriage. While pregnant with her second child, she expressed her feelings about her loss and her fears about loving the child she was carrying. To her first child she wrote,

> No one can know the painful, lonely loss I experienced at the center of my being when I lost you, little one. You had become my child; I held you within, longing for the moment I would hold you in my arms. . . . You will always be in my heart.

And she wrote to the child she was carrying:

> We love you so already. The excitement of your presence and future arrival grows with each passing day. Yes, I'm a little frightened. For in allowing myself to love you and

---

[1] © February 1986, "Miscarriage: Remnants of a Life," by Mary Davis. Reprinted with permission from *Marriage and Family Living* magazine (p. 16), Abbey Press. Saint Meinrad Arch Abbey, Saint Meinrad, IN 47577.
[2] Ibid.

anticipate your coming with joy, I am opening myself up to
the possibility of the deepest of pain should I lose you too.
I am giving myself to you for this very important time in
your development. I am enriched because you need me so
much, for a time. And I shall be here, for as long as you
need me to be, until you are able to move away at your own
pace in fulfillment of your life possibilities. . . . So keep
growing, little one. I'm anxious to see you, hold you, love
you, and care for you for as long as I'm allowed.

For some women, the decision to become pregnant again
does result in what they feared most—another loss. Repeated pregnancy losses are devastating. When you want
very much to be a mother, it is easy to feel like a failure
when you can't seem to produce a healthy child.

It is also frustrating that so many losses do not have
definitive reasons. And sometimes it seems women are sent
home and told to try again, with very little investigation
into the cause of their pregnancy failures. If you've experienced pregnancy loss, it is important that you have competent medical advice. You have the right to have your
questions answered as fully as possible (granted that there
are a lot of unknowns) and to have a doctor who is aware of
your history and sensitive to your concerns.

Sometimes it is difficult to make decisions about the future after a pregnancy loss. Nothing seems sure anymore.
You fear being pregnant again, and yet there is anger and
disappointment in not being pregnant.

If you take your struggles, your questions, your disappointments to God, you will find that he does care about
you. And you will begin to sense that there is a future for
you, even if it's not the future you planned for yourself. He
is the God who says, "I know the plans I have for you . . .
plans to prosper you and not to harm you, plans to give you
hope and a future" (Jer. 29:11, NIV). If you walk with him,
there will come a time when you can say as one woman did,
"I am beginning to be healed of my hurt and grief. I can

look to the future, even to a future which might not include a baby."[3]

## JOURNAL

What are your hopes for the future? What are your fears? Do you want another child? Are you afraid to be pregnant again? How do you feel about a future that might not include a baby born to you? What are your hopes and dreams for a baby that may be born to you?

[3]Ibid.

# 27. ONE YEAR LATER

Adding to my joy at being pregnant again was the fact that my friend, Joan, was pregnant at the same time. She was due in September, while I was due in December. Together we watched our bellies enlarge and shared the details of our pregnancies. Kathy listened and encouraged. The three of us went on a short trip together in July, as we knew it would be a long time before we could do it again. How I treasured their friendships!

As September approached, I wasn't prepared for my pensive thoughts and moods. I began to dwell on my pregnancy of the year before—my hopes, my anticipations, my loss. As the September 12 birthday of our child drew nearer, I battled depression. I realized anew that the child I was carrying would never replace the child we had lost.

On September 5, five days before her due date, Joan was admitted into the hospital and prepped for delivery. I stayed near the phone waiting for Kathy to call with a progress report from the hospital. Her report surprised me: Joan's rhythmic contractions had stopped, and she was sent home. Later the three of us laughed together and decided that her baby had another day in mind for a birthday.

The day before what would have been our child's birthday, the events of the year before ran through my head. I saw myself in my doctor's office, and I remembered the lighthearted trip to the hospital when I was so certain nothing was wrong. I recalled the doctor's solemn words and relived the late night labor. As I went to bed that night my thoughts were filled with the memory of the silent delivery room.

The phone rang at 4:00 A.M. It was Kathy. She was at the hospital with Joan, who was definitely in labor. Tears choked my voice. "Oh, Kathy, I knew this would happen. Can you believe it? The same day as our baby's birth." I babbled some more while Kathy listened with understanding. She shared my disbelief. She went on to tell me when the doctor thought Joan's baby would arrive. We had been given permission to watch the birth from the window of the delivery room.

Patrick was awakened by the phone and heard me speak. I hung up the receiver and rolled into his arms. I was astonished by my tears. My thoughts kept repeating themselves. "I had a baby on this date. This was my baby's birthday, too. But my baby died." It hurt. I didn't know it would hurt so much, especially since I was pregnant. I was amazed at the depth of my pain. It was as if it were happening all over again. I sobbed for several minutes while Patrick held me and comforted me.

After awhile, I showered and dressed to go to the hospital. I was thankful Joan was finally having her baby, but my own sadness competed with my joy for her. I shook my head in wonderment at God's timing. I comforted myself with the thought that special babies must be born on this date.

Kathy greeted me at the hospital with a hug and we planted ourselves in front of the tiny window. Joan's husband, Tom, was with her in the delivery room, as was his sister with her camera. Joan gave me a fleeting smile as our eyes met. As Kathy and I watched and waited, I was swept back once again to another delivery room exactly one year earlier. I was glad we didn't have to wait long before Joan and Tom's new son, Keegan, arrived. We all cried tears of joy. Intermingled with my tears of joy were tears of sadness and longing for a baby I had never known or held.


## REFLECTION

The calendar will be a constant reminder of your loss. If you lost your baby early in pregnancy, you may find yourself approaching your due date with dread. It is confirmation of your loss. The day you expected to be greeting a newborn with joy is just another empty day. There is no baby.

The anniversaries of your baby's birth and death are difficult days. Judy found herself reliving the events of the year before. Other women have also done that. Joanne writes:

Working up to the anniversary was very hard for me. So many memories came flashing back. Or we would be on a family outing, and I would look at my other three, and wonder how it would be to have Ethan there. What would he look like? What would his personality have been like? How would his presence have changed the dynamics of our family's life?

All of these questions and memories seem to intensify as the anniversary day nears. And no matter what you do, you cannot will that date off the calendar.

If you find yourself dreading the approach of the anniversary date or your expected due date, you may find it helpful to make specific plans for that day. You will be remembering your child that day anyway, so planning an activity of remembrance is appropriate. You may want to take flowers to the gravesite (if there is one), write a poem, send a donation to a favorite charity in your child's memory, or plant a tree. Choose an activity that is a meaningful commemoration for you of your child's life and death.

Then plan one activity that affirms *your* life. Do something that you enjoy, that makes you feel good about yourself. You may want to plan to spend time with a person who has supported you and listened to you during the past year. You will want to be with a person who realizes the importance of this day to you, and who won't ignore it. Above all give yourself time for remembering.

## JOURNAL

Is there a difficult day approaching for you? What do you dread about it? What can you plan to make it easier? What would you like to have happen that day? If you have already reached the milestone of the anniversary or due date, write about it. What was positive about the day? Is there anything you wish you had done differently?

# 28. AFTER SORROW COMES JOY

December came and I was brimming over with anticipation. The celebration of the birth of the Christ child enhanced the awe I felt for the miracle of life cradled within my womb. I looked forward to greeting Christmas morn with a newborn son in my arms. My days overflowed with preparations for Christmas, my parents' visit from Oregon, and readying the nursery. The official due date of December 12 spurred me on, even though I figured December 23 was more accurate. I hoped the baby would come just before then so I could be home with all the family for Christmas.

December 23 arrived, but still no baby. Patrick and I went to a nearby historic Spanish mission that afternoon for a strenuous hike up to the large wooden cross on the hill. It felt invigorating, but the only result was shortness of breath! We got back home just before my folks arrived. We were doubly excited to be together as we anticipated Christmas and the baby.

A delightful Christmas came and went. Dad returned to Oregon on the twenty-seventh, but Mom planned to stay a week past the baby's birth. I was disappointed Dad wouldn't get to see our son as a newborn. The next evening, contractions were strong and regular, and Patrick stayed home from his job in Goleta, only to have the contractions stop completely. I decided I'd be pregnant forever!

Regular contractions started once again just before dinner on December 30. I ate heartily of the delicious Reuben casserole Mom made, ignoring her caution, "Are you sure you want to eat that much if you're going into labor?" At that point I wasn't convinced the baby was ever coming and ignored her warnings.

Almost immediately after Patrick left for work, the contractions increased in intensity and regularity; soon I started to feel some pressure. I was surprised and puzzled. In my previous labors, I didn't feel pressure until the end when it was too intense to be ignored, but this seemed different. We left a message at Patrick's office for him to turn around and meet us at the hospital. I took a shower, a neighbor came to stay with the boys, and Kathy came to take Mom and me to the hospital.

Walking into the hospital, I had to stop with every contraction and do my breathing exercises. I maintained control just fine and wondered how many hours of labor I had ahead of me. After I'd changed into a white gown, a nurse checked me to see how far along I was. She became silent. I had a flashback to my previous labor and I fought back panic. I nearly asked her if everything was all right. Instead, I heard myself saying, "Well, how far along am I?"

Her puzzled expression matched her voice. "I don't see how it's possible, but I think you're complete." I hadn't heard the term "complete" before, and it took me a few seconds to realize I was dilated to ten centimeters. I was as astounded as she was.

My doctor soon arrived and confirmed that the nurse was right. I was ecstatic. All my prior labors had involved hours of strong contractions. I never dreamed it could be so easy. I breathed a prayer of thanks.

My doctor assured me it was safe to wait for Patrick since the bag of waters had not broken. We had shared the births of our other three children, and I didn't want him to miss this one. All the preparations were made, and I lay on the delivery table waiting for Patrick. Kathy stayed with me, encouraging me during the contractions and helping me with my breathing exercises. Joan came and so did our pastor. They waited with Mom outside the delivery room.

Once again the stage was set, this time with spectators. The contractions were getting harder, and I had just said, "I don't think I can wait any longer," when I heard a shout go up outside the room.

"He's here! He's here! Hurry up, Patrick!" As he pulled on his green hospital garb, he told us he had gone home to check on the kids before coming to the hospital. He, too, was accustomed to my slow labors. He walked into the delivery room at 10:58 and at 11:00 Kalen Patrick was born. Joy exploded inside me as fervent as Kalen's squalls. I had never heard such loud cries from a newborn—he only stopped to catch his breath for more cries. I had a glimpse of God smiling and saying to me, "I, too, remember the quiet delivery room. Here is my gift to you." Kalen's loud, lusty yells continued to fill the room. He finally quieted down a little when he was placed on my tummy.

Patrick hugged me, and I teased him about how easy he had gotten off this time as my labor coach. I felt fantastic. I didn't feel drained and exhausted as I had after the births of my other children. Instead, I was on top of the world. Some more friends were called, and they came to the hospital to celebrate with us. My room reverberated with our excitement.

Later, when Kalen was placed in my arms, I was overwhelmed with joy and gratitude. At last my arms held a precious newborn. As I admired him, I thanked God for the miracle of birth and for this perfect child. I sang to Kalen in a whisper the first words that came to me, "You are so beautiful to me," and I wept with joy.

## REFLECTION

Sorrow changed Judy. It thrust her out of her normal, complacent life and forced her into a world of suffering. Although she found the way of sorrow difficult, and often stumbled and fell, she emerged from the experience surprised at her own strength and with more confidence to face life.

Other women have also experienced the sense of strength that comes from living through the loss of a child. And they are able to face an uncertain future. Donna Moriarty, whose first pregnancy ended with the death of her daughter, wrote the following words:

> There is still the lurking fear of calamity, the seed of doubt that says there may never be another child. I hope that even if this were to happen—a horrible thought, but always a possibility—I will survive. I am stronger and wiser from this experience and, I like to think, a better candidate for motherhood than I was a year ago.[1]

Part of being able to look ahead is appreciating the gift of life now. Judy has found since her loss that she is much more aware of the fragility of life. Because of this she takes fewer things for granted and finds more reasons to celebrate. She has a deeper respect for her sons' lives and health and all that they are able to do. She treasures their "blown kisses" as she backs out of the driveway and their strong hugs when she comes home. She continually seeks to capture the joy of living.

Rediscovering joy was one of the surprising results of living through sorrow. Her sorrow carved a chasm that was deep and broad; the unexpected result was a deepened capacity for joy.

[1]Donna Moriarty, "The Right to Mourn," *Ms.*, November 1982, p. 82. Used by permission of the author.

The joy Judy felt after Kalen's birth was natural and normal. Yet it was deeper and richer than her joy at the birth of her other two sons. Kalen's birth did not erase the events of the year before. He could never replace the child she lost. But as her sorrow for that child had been deep, the height of her joy for Kalen was increased.

## JOURNAL

How has the sorrow of a failed pregnancy changed you? Are these changes positive or negative? How have you experienced joy in the months since your loss?

# 29. IN MEMORY OF . . .

Colorful "welcome home" signs plastered the front door when Kalen and I arrived home from the hospital. Lambs of every description decorated his cheery nursery. His brothers vied for turns to hold him. Cards and gifts from all over the country welcomed his arrival. Forty church women honored Kalen and me with a beautiful shower at a friend's home. Underlying the excitement over Kalen's birth was a deep sense of joy.

That same joy lightened the never-ending tasks of caring for a newborn. How good it was to nurse Kalen and stroke his fine, dark hair. Even the middle-of-the-night feedings rarely irritated me. Once I had rolled out of bed and shaken off the sleepiness, I anticipated returning to bed with Kalen nestled up to me. After bath time, I would enfold him in a soft baby quilt, then hold him close as I rocked him and made up lullabies using his name. Contentment and closeness wrapped around us as we cuddled together. I treasured those moments.

Yet in the midst of the joy of having a new baby in our home lingered the memory of the baby we never knew. I often wondered about the unknowns. How much did the baby weigh? Was it a boy or girl? I detested calling our child "it." I longed for an identity. I wondered if after further examining the baby the doctors had determined and recorded the sex. I questioned what should be done with the remains. The baby's ashes were all we had to indicate that I'd had a baby in September of 1979. I was troubled by a sense of unfinished business; the incompleteness nagged at me.

I tried to track down my hospital records, hoping they would offer some clues to my questions. Every effort was stymied; the doctor had moved, the records were elsewhere, and no one seemed to know or care where. I gave up easily. I felt energyless to pursue what might be nonexistent information.

A few months later, my doctor's nurse offered to help. I waited in anticipation, only to learn she had moved on to a different job. Disappointment prevailed. I resigned myself to never knowing any more. Another year went by.

Memories came flooding back when an Air Force couple in our church lost their baby four hours after birth in January of 1982. Vivacious Joanne and I had often talked together, and I was heartbroken for them. Patrick and I went to the graveside service along with other friends and family members. We huddled together against the cold wind. Just the sight of the tiny white casket brought tears to my eyes.

The short service was simple and touching. The words to the hymn couldn't get past the lump in my throat. I tried to control my tears. How I hurt for Scott and Joanne! Yet, deep down I knew the torrent of tears I was holding back was also for me. The "if onlys" paraded across my mind and haunted me once again. If only we had known the sex of our child, if only it had a name, if only we could have had a service for our precious baby. If only we had a place to go back to and remember. I felt cheated. The gap in my heart tore anew and I yearned for healing.

A couple of months later, a part-time job at a florist shop fell into my lap. One day while delivering flowers to the cemetery, I came across the section for babies' graves. I was astounded at how many there were. The rows went on and on. Was it possible that so many other parents had known sorrow like ours?

As my eyes skimmed the inscriptions on the markers, I flinched in pain—"Our darling," "Our little angel," "So much love, so little time." Often it was a simple "Our son" or "Our daughter." With each reading my pain multiplied; the intensity of it was suffocating. Tears blinded me as I walked on. Beneath the pain surfaced the unrelenting desire to know more about our child. As I drove away, I determined again to find out more.

At Kalen's next checkup, I met the new nurse. Sharon's congenial smile welcomed me, and we were soon chatting comfortably. She played with Kalen while checking his height and weight. Somehow the conversation turned to our previous baby. I sensed Sharon's caring, and soon my frustrations spilled out as I told her about my failure to locate the records and what I hoped to find.

"Let me see if I can get them for you." Her offer was immediate and sincere. I thanked her, and she promised she would call as soon as she knew anything. My steps matched the lightness in my heart as I left. I tried not to think about it as the days passed. Disappointment was too familiar.

When I returned home from work one day, Patrick's words grabbed me. "Sharon called today." He paused.

"Well, did she get the records?"

"Yes."

My heart was in my throat. "Did they say what the baby was?"

Patrick looked at me intently and quietly replied, "It was a girl."

The words exploded in my head and shot joy all through me. A daughter! We actually had a daughter! Just as quickly my elation vanished and was replaced with profound sorrow. "And we never knew her," I thought sadly. "We never knew her." Tears filled my eyes.

The next few days teemed with new thoughts and conversations. Patrick and I couldn't believe it was a girl. Having had only boys, we were amazed we could have anything else! I wanted to announce to the world, "It's a girl! It's a girl!" Instead, we shared the belated news with our families and closest friends.

We also learned from the records that our daughter weighed just under four pounds. I pictured her tiny face again and marveled at how large I had gotten when I carried her. Patrick and I discussed what we should do with the baby's ashes now that we had an identity. I talked with the director of the mortuary who also owned the flower shop where I worked. He was helpful and understanding. We decided to have a memorial service and bury her remains at the cemetery. A part of me felt foolish. Wasn't it a bit ridiculous to be doing this three years late? After all, what would people think? Surely they wouldn't understand. I finally realized these misgivings were unimportant; I knew I needed to do it.

Patrick offered to make a box for our baby's remains. He labored for hours at his workbench in the garage, carefully fashioning the box out of oak. The first time I saw it, tears sprang up in my eyes . . . her one earthly gift from her daddy.

I spent hours perusing the baby name books trying to decide on the perfect name, the one thing I could give her. We had not decided on names before she was born or I would have probably used that choice. It seemed strange, yet right, to be choosing a name for our child even three years after her birth. With Patrick's approval, I settled on a simple name, Ann Marie. I had always liked my middle name of Ann. I chose our daughter's name on what would have been her third birthday, September 12, 1982.

All that remained was to plan the memorial service. After considering different possibilities, Patrick and I agreed we wanted it to be an intimate, special time. Since we had no extended family living nearby, we decided to limit it to our immediate family. Pastor Tom was understanding of our desires and warmly consented to lead the service for us.

We set the date for September 15. My mind turned back to that day three years earlier when I had been overwhelmed with pain and sorrow. "How ironic," I thought, "that a date so filled with anguish can now also be remembered as a time filled with healing."

The day of the service dawned unusually cool and cloudy. I chose to wear a favorite long-sleeved, blue dress. When the rain began, I wryly thought, "How appropriate for a funeral. I can't believe this—it never rains here in September!" We picked up Travis and Kyle at their two different schools and headed up the hill to the cemetery. Pastor Tom and the funeral director were ready for us. At my request Ann Marie's gravesite was next to that of Scott and Joanne's son, Ethan. The beautiful oak box and a lovely bouquet my parents had sent lay between Tom and us. The boys, Patrick, and I each placed a pink sweetheart rose on her grave.

Patrick held Kalen while Kyle and Travis stood soberly next to us. I rested my hands on their shoulders. The wind whipped at my dress and hair as Tom began to speak. Light sprinkles of rain fell. As I listened to the words of Scripture and comfort, my tears joined the rain. I had wondered if I would cry. Yet these tears were different, for intermingled with the sorrow was joy. It was as if a healing balm were being rubbed all over my heart. Peace flooded my inner being. Any misgivings I had had concerning this belated service melted away. Even I hadn't fully realized how right and necessary it was. As Tom read Psalm 18:30, "As for God, his way is perfect . . ." (NIV), I was anointed with comfort and a sense of completion.

### REFLECTION

As much as Judy enjoyed Kalen, his presence didn't make her forget the baby she had lost. There were so many unanswered questions. A box of ashes sat in the back of her desk drawer with no permanent place. She felt a nagging sense of incompleteness.

The funeral service for Scott and Joanne's newborn son, Ethan, made her realize what she needed to do to put the active mourning for her child behind her. She needed to find the information to answer her questions about the sex, the size, and the disabilities of her baby. And she needed a memorial service for her child.

Judy's search for information was sporadic, with lots of stops and starts. She was busy with a new baby and then a new job. But shortly before the third anniversary of her baby's birth and death, she received the information she needed. She had had a girl. With that knowledge she began to think about a name for the baby and a way to say good-bye.

When Ann Marie was born, Judy and Patrick were not given a range of choices about the disposition of her body. They ended up with a cardboard box of ashes and had no idea what to do with them. Once their child had more of an identity—had a sex and a name, burying her remains in their local cemetery seemed right to them.

Decisions about whether to name and whether to bury the child are decisions that most couples make in the first few hours after their loss. They are difficult decisions with no right or wrong answers. Couples need to talk about what best fits their needs and do what seems right to them. There are choices, and if those who have lost a baby don't feel comfortable with the alternatives offered by the funeral home or the hospital, they can ask for information about other available options.

Many couples decide to name the child that doesn't live. It helps give that child an identity. Others choose not to. When Kim and Jim lost their son in the fifth month of Kim's pregnancy, they hadn't picked out a name yet, and decided not to name him, because as Kim says, "We didn't want to just stick a name on him." Others, like Judy, find the giving of a name to be one of the few things they can do for their child and they want to do it. It's a highly personal choice.

Kim and Jim had their son cremated, and his ashes were spread in a special rose garden maintained by the mortuary for babies' ashes. Kim also collected all the cards they received after his death and put them in a baby book. She put all the ribbons from floral arrangements in the book, along with pictures of the arrangements. Working on the book, remembering her son's short life, was part of her grieving and a step in her healing.

Scott and Joanne have in their home what they call "Ethan's Wall." That wall is reserved for anything to do with Ethan—framed special cards, poems that loved ones have written—all are in memory of Ethan. It's their place for remembering their son.

Karen and Paul also found that "healing comes from remembering." They thought of their baby often and looked at his picture and footprints. They added his name to the "We Love You, Mommy" plaque on their wall. And they considered their family a family with four children—three living with them now and one living in heaven with Jesus.

In the early stages of grief, it is important to remember the event of loss and experience all of the feelings associated with it. One of the paradoxes of grieving is that those who remember well, who experience the pain of their loss deeply, are able to let go of the grief more easily. Those who fight the pain, and try not to remember what happened, have a harder time letting go of their grief.

Remembering, knowing what you've lost, is important in the early days of grief. But as time passes, you may realize that you are ready to say good-bye. This doesn't mean that you forget about what happened or that you forget your child. It does mean that you're ready to let go of your grief and begin to more actively live your own life again.

Some find that grief gradually diminishes until it is no longer an active part of their lives. Others seem to need a more active way to "finish" their grief. Unfortunately, our society offers no ceremonies or rituals for the ending of grief. For Judy, the graveside service became a ritual of letting go. Getting Ann Marie's remains out of the desk, out of the house, and committing them to the ground was for Judy a very active and concrete way of letting go of this child and of her grief over her death.

If you find yourself seeking to let go, but not knowing how to do it, you might consider writing a letter to the child you lost. In your letter you might want to tell the child the circumstances of your pregnancy, what you were anticipating, and your feelings when the pregnancy failed. You might also include how this experience has changed you and what your hopes are for the future. When you've finished writing to your child, read the letter out loud.

Letting go, saying good-bye, does not mean that you never think of that child again with sadness or that you're no longer reminded of your loss. It just means that your loss is no longer the most important part of your identity and that you're ready to move on with your life. Your loss experience was an important chapter in your life, and it will always have an impact on the succeeding chapters of your life.

## JOURNAL

How have you "remembered" your child? Are you feeling ready to let go and say good-bye to your child? Does writing a letter to your child appeal to you, or do you have another way of saying good-bye?

Listen carefully to your feelings, and do what seems right for you. Don't try to do this exercise too soon after your loss. Give yourself plenty of time.

# 30. FROM MOURNING TO MINISTRY

Shortly after our baby's death, a thought slipped in between the layers of sorrow and pain that had encased me. "Someday good will come out of this." The message glimmered only a moment and, to my relief, soon faded away. How could good possibly come out of this heartbreak? I couldn't imagine. All I could see or hear or feel at that time was pain. I saw no good in my loss; it hurt terribly. As the weeks moved into months and the pain gradually eased, I welcomed the possibility of good coming out of my loss. Now with the perspective of several years, I am amazed and humbled at how God has used my loss to extend his comfort to others.

God began using my experience in the lives of others within the first year of our baby's birth and death. I had been attending the local Christian Women's Club since we moved back to Lompoc. I enjoyed the luncheon, visiting with other women, and the program, which included a speaker from out of town. The speakers' life stories fascinated me, and I always marveled at how God had worked in their lives.

Through a mutual friend I became acquainted with Linda, who was president of the club. Her warm smile and sparkly eyes made conversation easy when we occasionally saw each other. I was curious when she phoned me one day but assumed she needed something done for the upcoming luncheon. I wasn't prepared for her question. "Judy, would you be willing to be a speaker for Christian Women's Clubs? We are having a workshop in Ventura to train speakers, and I would like you to come."

A no was traveling quickly from my heart to my mouth, but I caught it just in time. I promised her I would think and pray about it. I hung up wondering why I had swallowed my initial response. How could I even consider speaking? I knew the bulk of my story would be sharing the loss of our baby. How could I talk about that without crying? Besides, I was still in my twenties. What could I possibly say that the older women could relate to? They should be sharing their stories, not me.

I flung my thoughts up to God, hoping he would agree. I reluctantly kept my promise and prayed about going to the speakers' workshop. God's nudging was a clear yes. I resisted his answer and reminded him of all my objections. The yes remained. I consoled myself with the thought that maybe I was just supposed to go to the workshop and that it wouldn't result in my ever speaking.

After the workshop and many scribbled pages, tears, and prayers later, I found myself standing in front of our Lompoc Christian Women's Club telling my story. Eight months pregnant with Kalen and wearing a borrowed orange outfit, I referred to myself as "The Great Pumpkin." Joan and Kathy encouraged me with their smiles and their eyes, and I knew they were praying for me. Other church friends were doing the same. As I spoke, I was so aware of God's help and his calming presence.

Before the luncheon I had prayed that at least one woman would invite Christ into her life. I was thrilled when four women responded to the invitation to receive Christ. Afterward Joan and I went to Kathy's house, where our relief and excitement overflowed. With tears in her eyes, Joan leaned toward me. "Just think, Judy. Your baby's short life has already helped lead four people into God's kingdom." My tears joined hers.

I didn't speak for club groups again until after Kalen was born. Since then, I have spoken to many clubs in California. God's perfect timing never fails to amaze me. After one meeting, a woman grabbed my hands and with tears choking her voice said, "I'm from Anchorage, Alaska, and I know God brought me here to hear you. I've lost two babies, and what you said really helped me."

When I spoke in Bakersfield, a petite, attractive woman approached me afterward and tears filled her eyes as she spoke. "I had a similar experience to yours, but worse. I've been thinking about speaking for Christian Women's Clubs, but how do you talk about it without crying?" I told her that sometimes I did cry when I spoke, and I encouraged her to tell me her story.

My heart broke as she told me of their son. He had lived six days, but she never even saw her baby. We talked for a long time, and as we were leaving, she said, "Our baby died two and a half years ago, and you're the first person I've talked to who understands." Cathie and I exchanged addresses, and I later wrote her, encouraging her to name their son and have a memorial service for him. This they did, and she, too, experienced a beautiful healing of her grief.

I worked part time for over two years in a flower shop that was next-door to a mortuary. Occasionally I dealt with distraught customers trying to decide on flowers for a funeral. One woman couldn't contain her sobbing, and I stood and held her hands in mine as she poured out her grief. A fellow employee told me, "I'm so glad you were here; I just couldn't have handled that."

Another time a man came in to order roses for his wife. I wondered if they were for a special occasion, and I nearly asked him but didn't. Yet, as if I *had* asked, he told me that the reason for his getting the roses was a sad one. "My wife was six-months pregnant and our baby died today." His words pierced my own wound, and I felt their fresh pain. After expressing my sympathy, I related to him some of our experience and encouraged him to talk. By the time I finished his order, we had arranged for me to go and see his wife.

When I entered their apartment, the relatives discreetly disappeared, and I met his lovely, dark-haired wife. An immediate bond linked our hearts. I leaned toward her as she told me how excited they had been about this, their second child. She described their shock and disappointment. She mentioned that her grandmother was planning to come that Christmas, and they had been looking forward to having their newborn there for her to see. I nodded my head, remembering my own expectations of having a new baby at Christmas time. How special it was for me to give her the gift of listening as Joan and Kathy had done for me. That Christmas I received a beautiful card from her thanking me again for coming and saying how much it had meant to her to talk to someone who understood.

Since we lost Ann Marie, several women in our church have experienced pregnancy loss. My heart breaks each time. Shortly after my friend Joanne's baby died, they were transferred to Ohio. No one there knew she had just had a baby that died. Often Joanne would call just because she needed to talk to someone who had been there. "Did you feel this way?" she would question. "Are these feelings normal?" Often she'd say, "Oh, I feel so much better after talking to you." Our shared tears often turned to laughter by the end of the conversation.

I met Betsy shortly after Kalen was born. She and her husband, Jim, had recently moved in a couple of blocks away from us. As our friendship grew, she shared with me her deep longing for a child. Betsy was eagerly anticipating the time when her husband's schooling would be finished and they could start their family. As I watched her play with and delight in Kalen, I shared her anticipation.

I shouted with joy when she told me she was pregnant. At last! She bubbled with excitement and expectancy. Several weeks later she called one night and in a flat voice told me she had miscarried. My balloon of joy deflated along with hers. How I hurt for her.

"Oh, Betsy, I am so sorry." Sadness bound us as she explained how it had happened. I groped for comforting words. "Well, Betsy, the Lord knows just when the right time is." After a couple more platitudes, I stopped in midsentence. "Oh, Betsy, forgive me. Here I am trying to make you feel better. That's just what people did to me and I hated it!"

"That's OK, Judy. You're right, it doesn't help."

When she became pregnant again, our joy returned, subdued by caution. And disappointment dampened our joy because she and Jim would be moving to Nebraska before the baby was born. Many friends gathered for a delightful shower just a few weeks before they moved. Cameras flashed often as Betsy oohed and aahed over every gift.

After their move, we talked on the phone as her due date edged closer. We giggled together as she described how big she was getting. Betsy was always so tiny; it was hard to picture that much roundness on her petite frame. She promised to call as soon as possible after the birth.

A few days past Betsy's due date, a mutual friend called and told me the baby had died in the womb. My heart wrenched with pain—not again! I cried and cried, overwhelmed by sorrow. I called her after the delivery. More tears. She told me, "Judy, I've remembered everything you said." She recounted how she and Jim had held their son and taken pictures. And Jim had written the memorial service.

My mind went back to the days when Betsy and I jogged together. During our leisurely runs, I had shared much of Ann Marie's story. I had reviewed with Betsy all the things I would have done differently if I had only known to do them. Mingled with my sorrow now was thankfulness that my sad experience had helped them avoid additional regrets.

Unfortunately, the calls never end. Just a few weeks ago, I received a call at work from our church secretary. Tearfully, she told me that her son's wife, who was seven months along, had just lost their baby. Sadness washed over me. Beth and I often sat near each other in church, and we usually chatted about the expected baby, their second.

Unable to concentrate on work, I left a few minutes early and went to see Beth and her husband at the hospital. I knew words were inadequate, but I just wanted to be there with them. They told me they were uncertain what to do about a funeral. I briefly told them about our delayed memorial service. Later that day I sent a plant, along with a booklet, *When Hello Means Goodbye*,[1] that gives suggestions for parents suffering from pregnancy loss.

Prompted by one of the suggestions, she and her husband requested a birth certificate for their daughter. Beth was pleased that it was "just like Allison's," their firstborn. "We would have never known to do it if we hadn't read about it. And because of the certificate, we also learned her weight and length." They named their daughter Ashley Elizabeth, and had a private memorial service for her.

Before my loss, I was uncomfortable with grief. When someone I knew lost a loved one, I would send a card with a brief note, never knowing exactly what to say or do. Feeling awkward, I shied away from them. I wanted to help, but I didn't know how.

I have since learned there isn't a lot that needs to be said, but there is much that needs to be listened to with love and understanding. I try to offer that along with a hug. I remember what helped me, and I pray for wisdom to respond appropriately in each new situation. I never want to completely forget the pain and sadness I experienced so that I can better minister to those who are hurting.

---

[1]Pat Schwiebert, R.N., and Paul Kirk, M.D., *When Hello Means Goodbye* (Portland, OR: University of Oregon Health Sciences Center, 1981).

## REFLECTION

In the early days after her loss, Judy would not have dreamed that in a little over a year she would be standing in front of the Christian Women's Club telling her story. She had no idea that she would someday be comforting distraught customers in a florist's shop. She was able to do these things because she wanted to share with others some of what she had learned on her journey with grief. And she wanted some good to come out of her experiences.

Cathie's meeting Judy at a Christian Women's Club luncheon in Bakersfield was a significant turning point in her life. By talking with Judy, Cathie was able to take steps that helped her resolve her grief. Then she decided that she needed to do something for other women in her city who experienced pregnancy loss. She writes,

> When we were preparing for our child's belated memorial service, I pulled out of my records a letter from our pediatrician, which included the scripture 2 Corinthians 1:3–4: "Blessed be the God and Father of our Lord Jesus Christ, the Father of mercies and God of all comfort; who comforts us in all our affliction so that we may be able to comfort those who are in any affliction with the comfort with which we ourselves are comforted by God" (NASB).

> Reading that letter that day, I felt God was talking just to me. Judy was using her tragedy for good by speaking to Christian Women's Clubs. I felt the good that God wanted to come out of my loss was for me to be able to comfort others who were also losing babies. After all, I had allowed my grief to go on for three years before I had resolved it— partly due to the poor advice I had received in the hospital.

> I decided that if I could start a support group and give parents some information on infant loss while they were still in the hospital, they might have a better idea of what to do. They would be able to ask for a birth certificate, pictures, and other mementos before they left. They would be

able to choose what to do with the body, rather than just allowing the hospital to dispose of the baby. And they would know it's not weird or abnormal to want a funeral for the baby.

I went to my pediatrician with the booklet Judy sent me, *When Hello Means Goodbye,* and told him what I wanted to do. He was encouraging, and not long after that his office put me in touch with the mother of a baby who had recently died. We got together and shared our experiences. Little by little, word got out that we were interested in starting a support group, and the Lord led four other women into the group.

Today we have monthly meetings that include both husbands and wives. We've raised money and started a lending library on pregnancy loss. We have given information to the hospitals and can proudly say that things are handled better there now. As soon as a problem pregnancy is discovered, the patient's room is marked from the outside so that anyone entering knows that all is not well. In addition, the hospital hands out one of our calling cards and a booklet for the parents to read while they're still in the hospital. This does not relieve the parents of their pain, but it certainly does make a difference in the resolution of their grief.

And so the chain of comfort grows—from Judy, to Cathie, to many other women. When you've walked through grief, you have a much better idea of how to help someone in grief than does someone who has never known sorrow.

Although you would never ask to have the experience of losing a child, using your experience to help others is a way of giving meaning to the event. And it enables you to see the truth of the idea that when God is present in our lives, no experience is wasted. If you are able to give comfort and support to someone else facing grief and loss, your loss has not been for nothing. And if, over time, you are able to encourage your sorrowing friend to reach out to someone else—to continue the chain of comfort—the love and grace you experienced in your loss will be passed on.

## JOURNAL

Has there been someone who comforted you out of her (or his) own experience with grief? Have you had opportunities to comfort anyone else? Do you see any opportunities for ministry coming out of your loss experience?

# 31. ALWAYS REMINDERS

Several years later, I am still often reminded of a little girl named Ann Marie. Mention of the year 1979 triggers memories and I will recall, "I was pregnant with Ann Marie then," or "That was right after Ann Marie died." When I hear or read her name, my heart contracts again and I remember.

A few years after her death, I went back to the hospital where she was born and talked with the nurse who had been with me during the delivery. I shared with her that we had named our baby and held a belated memorial service.

"What did you name her?" she asked.

"Ann Marie."

She caught her breath and squeezed my arm. "My oldest daughter is named Ann Marie."

With tears glistening in our eyes, we looked at each other in disbelief.

If Ann Marie had lived, she would have been in fourth grade this year. I think of that sometimes when I read stories to the fourth graders when they come to the school library where I work. Some of the students are especially close to my heart.

Little Laurel, for example, born just three days after Ann Marie, has a special spot in my heart. I met her and her parents at our church on Easter Sunday when she was seven months old. I have delighted in watching her over the years; it's an added joy to check out to her such books as *Charlotte's Web*.

Then there's Kelly. From the beginning of the year at our newly opened school, I found notes written on bookmarks tucked in her returned books. In her neat printing, she tells me how much she liked that week's book and why. She has typed me notes, drawn me pictures, and has made me special cards and gifts. Each one is signed "Love, Kelly J."

I was delighted later when I met her mother, Melanie. I expressed to her how special Kelly is to me. (Later, through an unusual, yet God-directed chain of events, Melanie typed the final draft of this book manuscript.) We were amazed when we realized that Kelly and Ann Marie had been born in the same hospital—and that I had nearly given our daughter the name of Kelly.

Two other girls in the fourth grade come from difficult home situations. Plagued with problems, they come to me for a hug or smile. As one of them left the library yesterday, she stopped at the door and looked back at me. Flashing me a big smile, she called out, "Love you!" and was gone. Being with these girls gives me a taste of what might have been.

Ann Marie's birthday is my most poignant reminder of her. Often on that day I have been at Keegan's birthday celebration, and I imagine what Ann Marie's party would have been like. My mind wanders as I try to picture her . . . what would she have chosen to wear for her party, a frilly dress or jeans? What kind of cake would she have requested? What would be her favorite flavor of ice cream? What would we have bought her for her special day? I wonder . . . are there birthday parties in heaven?

Instead of wrapping gifts or decorating her birthday cake, I take pink carnations, daisies, or sweetheart roses to her grave. And I remember her sweet little face and the promise of heaven. The remembering is bittersweet as I ponder all she has taught me with her brief life and how many lives have been touched through hers.

Her birthday passes unnoticed by nearly everyone else, but Joanne remembers every year. Whether the Air Force has them stationed in Alaska or Ohio, she always calls on that day and lets me know she's thinking of us. For she, too, had a baby that died and she understands. We share an inseparable bond.

When meeting someone for the first time, they usually ask about my children. I respond, "I have three sons." I inwardly brace myself for the inevitable next question. "No girls, huh?" or "Aren't you going to try for a girl?"

I would like to answer them correctly the first time with, "We have three boys and one girl, but our daughter died at birth." Instead, not wanting to make them uncomfortable, I respond, "No, no girls." And inside I treasure the knowledge that we have a daughter in heaven.

During the years when we didn't have an identity for our child, coupled with the fact we knew our baby was in heaven, I often thought of her as "our little angel." Every Christmas I buy a special ornament for our boys; in recent years I have bought angel ornaments to hang in memory of Ann Marie. Just as I do with our sons' ornaments, I write her name and the year on the ornament. It's just a small thing, but it's another concrete way to acknowledge her life.

I realize there will always be reminders. Some will continue, such as the first day of school—each year I think about what grade she would be in. I imagine that will go on until her possible graduation from college. And I wouldn't be surprised if someday there will be a girlfriend or possibly a wife of one of our sons who was born close to Ann Marie's birthday or who maybe shares her name. Glimpses of braids, mother-daughter functions, the holidays—each one tugs at my heart and I think of our daughter. For her birth and death were a significant chapter in my life that will forever be a part of me . . . and I'll always remember.

## REFLECTION

Your life has more or less returned to normal. You are no longer actively grieving. Yet, once in a while you are reminded of your loss and find yourself responding to situations with surprising intensity. Or you feel overwhelmed by sadness for a short time. These feelings surprise you; you thought you were through grieving.

Joanne experienced strong feelings about Ethan several years after his death, particularly around the date of his birth. She relates the following:

> I wasn't walking around the house crying like I had at the first, but there were still times, when out of the blue, the pain would well up, tears would overflow, and I would ache for my baby.

Joanne was reassured after a talk with her mother-in-law, who had lost a baby girl a year before Joanne's husband was born. Her mother-in-law told her that even up to twenty-two years after the loss of her daughter, she would take flowers to the grave or send money to some charity to commemorate her birth.

Because of your loss, there is a gap in your life. And even though you may have finished grieving, you will still be in situations that will remind you of your loss and fill you with sadness for what might have been. Your feelings show that you're human and you recognize what you've lost. They don't mean that you haven't essentially finished the grieving process. As Kim says,

> Time does help. The hours slowly turn into days, the days finally turn into months, and the months drag into years. The raw wounds close over very tenderly. The hurt becomes less vulnerable to everyday stresses, but it never loses its impact on your life. You have been forever changed.

## JOURNAL

Have you been caught off guard by feelings of grief months or even years after your loss? What events triggered your feelings? Are there questions about your family, such as "How many children do you have?" that you find difficult to answer? What are the most poignant reminders of your child?

# 32. LIVING WITH THE QUESTIONS

Why did our baby die? In the weeks and months after the birth and death of our baby, that question and others lurked in the recesses of my mind. At first I didn't think I should actively voice any questions. Wouldn't that be doubting God and his wisdom? Shouldn't I just accept what had happened and not question God's ways? So I attempted to bottle up my questions and go on with my life.

But my questions refused to go away. The "whys?" would often spring up unexpectedly to taunt me. Citing the medical reasons for our baby's death didn't satisfy me. It just led to other questions such as, "Why did our baby even have so many problems that she died?"

In some ways I felt fortunate. At least I had a medical explanation for our baby's death. Other parents I knew didn't even have that. Seemingly healthy babies died and the cause was never known. But why does it happen? Why does the cord wrap itself around a healthy baby's neck causing him to die? I found myself suddenly immersed in the world of human suffering. The subjects of my questions expanded with each day's headlines. As I heard of each new loss and fresh pain, the question why pulsated within me. Yet the answer I most desired was to my own plaintive why.

After our baby's death, I often heard variations on the theme, "It must have been God's will."

"God's will?" I screamed inside. "God's will for an innocent child to die? How can you say such a thing?"

That statement painted a portrait for me of a heartless, unfeeling God. It contrasted sharply with the character of the God I had known as my best friend since childhood. I realized that he allowed our child's death, but I refused to believe that he planned it that way and willed it to be. I could barely handle the fact that he allowed it. I questioned, wondered, and didn't understand. Why my child? Why not the child of an unwed mother who hadn't even wanted a child? Why? Why? Why?

After the January night when I threw my anger and questions at God, I felt I had his permission to be real with him. And my conversations with God continued to be peppered with questions—honest questions filled with pain, anger, and distress. Never did I feel that God was shirking from them. Rather, I sensed his love and understanding. I rarely received answers, but how good it was to learn that he could handle my questions. And more than that, I sensed his invitation to crawl up on his lap for his love and comfort.

Now when someone tells me, "We have no right to question God," I disagree. I'm still taking my questions to God.

Recently a friend who teaches at the school where I work miscarried on Christmas day. The entire staff had rejoiced with Teri when we learned of her pregnancy. My heart sank when she told me the sad news. I hugged her and we cried together.

*Why Teri?* I thought. She was so excited over this, her first pregnancy. As she told me her story, I felt her pain—"It happened right as we sat down to Christmas dinner"—and her devastation—"I feel like a part of me has been stripped away." And I heard her whys.

After her miscarriage, Teri had attended a family reunion where a younger cousin was present with her ten-month-old son. Teri eyed him from afar and held him only briefly.

"I know that baby wasn't planned," she said, "and I couldn't help wondering, why did her baby live and mine didn't?" I shook my head with her. Why, indeed?

During library time recently, I read *A Taste of Blackberries* to the fourth and fifth grade classes. Several students pestered me to read the book to them after I told them it had made me cry. It's a poignant story of a boy dealing with the death of his best friend from an allergic reaction to bee stings. The day after his friend's death, he wanders into the backyard garden of his next door neighbor, an elderly woman named Mrs. Mullins. They begin to talk:

> "You know about Jamie?"
> "Yes. I am so sorry about Jamie. And sorry about you, too, because you were his friend."
>
> . . . . . .
>
> "Why did he have to die?" The question lay there in the air between us. The sound of it shocked me, but Mrs. Mullins didn't act surprised.
> "Honey, one of the hardest things we have to learn is that some questions do not have answers." I nodded. This made more sense than if she tried to tell me some junk about God needing angels.[1]

As I read this story seven years after the loss of our baby, Mrs. Mullins's simple statement wrapped one more layer of comfort around me. "Honey, one of the hardest things we have to learn is that some questions do not have answers." It beautifully expressed for me what I, too, had painfully learned. There were no answers to my whys. My questions remained, but my wrestling for answers gradually diminished and finally stopped.

In place of concrete answers, I found steadying comforts. In the silence after my questions, I heard God's strong, yet tender response, "Trust me." And as I have lifted my pain and questions to a trustworthy God, I have

---

[1] Doris Smith, *A Taste of Blackberries* (New York: Crowell, 1978), p. 43.

watched him take them and use them to weave healing into my life and the lives of others. Even when there seem to be no answers, God has always been right there with me, and his unfailing presence has made it possible for me to live with the questions.

## REFLECTION

Very early in her experience, Judy's mom shared a verse with her that brought her comfort. "As for God, his way is perfect . . ." (Ps. 18:30, NIV). Judy believed that. She knew that. Yet, she couldn't wholeheartedly assent to that until she had struggled with her questions. Until she had felt her hurt and her anger. Until she realized how limited and human she was.

When she tried to bypass her pain and her questions, her acceptance wasn't authentic. It was superficial, and it left huge areas of her life that were closed—closed to herself and closed to God. Because deep down there were feelings and thoughts that she hadn't come to terms with.

Judy was never really tempted to blame God for her misfortune. But many people do. Often it's because they expect everything to go the way they want it to go. If they are trying to follow God, then often blessings are expected to follow. When a pregnancy fails instead of producing the new life that was expected, some blame God. They say, "If God loved me, he wouldn't have let this happen."

If anything, early in her experience, Judy chose to "protect" God. She wouldn't bring him her hard questions. As the pain eased, she began to look for some good to come out of her tragedy. Surely God had a reason for this happening—all she had to do was figure it out.

As time went on, she learned that she could take her questions to God and wrestle with him about the whys of her loss and the whys of human suffering. For all at once she was aware of the suffering of the world in a way that she had never been before. It was almost over-whelming.

Judy discovered as she took her anger, pain, and ques-tions to God that he was bigger than all of them. And he loved her in spite of them, maybe even because of them. She learned that she didn't have to be perfect or have her theology all figured out in order to be with God. She learned that he loved her and accepted her just the way she was—confused, hurt, and angry.

As her relationship with God grew, she realized that this relationship was the essence of her faith. God had called her into a relationship with him. She couldn't ever earn it, but through Jesus it was a gift. All she had to do was be with him. And as she was with him, she learned more and more that their relationship was based on God's steadfast love for her—a love that never wavered, never changed. And when she believed that, she realized that she could accept what had happened to her because she knew she was loved.

Judy still doesn't have the answers to all her questions. Like many other Christians, she still struggles with evil in the world and God's role in the battle. But she would agree with Kim, who says,

> There will always be questions of "what if?" But there are no pat answers. Only God's love can soothe this hurtfulness out of your spirit.

And she would feel a oneness of spirit with Karen and Paul, whose fourth child died before birth. Paul wrote:

> We do not believe that God's perfect plan includes chil-dren dying in the womb. He is sovereign and does what pleases him, but he came to bring life, not death. We live, however, in a broken world that is shot through with suf-fering and death. It is consoling to know that God not only rules—he also overrules. That which may not have been

part of the plan, he can still weave into the tapestry of his holy will for us. We cannot say whether God purposed this or allowed it. But behind everything—even sin, death, and the Devil himself—is an omniscient, compassionate God, Creator of the universe, and Lord over the living and the dead.

Tragedy and loss bring us face to face with the limits of our power as humans. No matter how badly we want some things, we cannot, by the power of our will or our hard work or our good life, make them happen. In many ways we are very helpless. But we don't like to feel helpless, and so we expend a great deal of effort and energy in activities that make us feel powerful and in control. Tragedy shatters illusions about any power that we may have.

And tragedy brings us face to face with the limits of our understanding. We just don't know why tragedies occur, and we probably never will. That is hard to accept. So we can keep wrestling with the questions, searching for the ever more elusive answers; or we can begin to see that there are some questions that don't have answers. Or at least they don't have answers we can comprehend.

Still, our struggle is worthwhile, for it is through our struggle that we begin to accept what has happened. We come to a truer understanding of ourselves—both our strengths and our weaknesses. And we can come to a deeper and truer relationship with God, who calls us to follow him. And because of that relationship, it is possible to live with the unanswered questions and face the rest of life with confidence.

## JOURNAL

What are the questions you have about your loss, the questions for which there don't seem to be answers? Has it been easy or hard for you to live with these questions? Is it easy or difficult for you to accept that "some questions do not have answers?"

Has your struggle with your questions brought you closer to or further away from God? If it seems that God is very distant (and this often happens), how do you feel about that? On the other hand, you may have experienced God in a new way through this experience. Write in your journal what this experience of loss has taught you about God.

# EPILOGUE

September 14, 1986

We went to the cemetery this afternoon. Ann Marie would have been seven two days ago. Even though the grave marker has been here for four years, today is the first time the five of us have gone together.

I took with us a couple of big bunches of daisies I had bought the day before. The cemetery was nearly deserted, and the sunny afternoon cradled us with a gentle breeze. I knelt in front of Ann Marie's marker and brushed away the clinging leaves and dead grass. Kalen helped me. We did the same for the adjacent marker of our friends' son, Ethan. Travis dumped stale water and faded flowers out of the flower containers and ran to get fresh water.

Patrick stretched out on his side, and each one of the boys found "his" spot on the grass. Peacefulness caressed us.

I had begun carefully cutting each daisy stem to the right length and placing them in the water when Kyle popped up with, "Hey, Mom, don't we get to put some in?"

His request startled and pleased me. "Of course. Here's a stem for each of you."

After handing daisies to the boys, I reached over to give one to Patrick. He waved it away saying, "That's OK. I don't need one." I sensed he didn't want to deprive someone else of putting it in.

Travis jumped in immediately. "Yes, Dad, you take one, too. Come on, Dad." Patrick smiled at Travis's insistence and reached for the blossom.

I put some flowers in both Ann Marie's and Ethan's containers. We talked as I arranged the flowers and fern fronds.

"I wonder if she's still a baby or if she's seven years old."

"Do you think we'd recognize her if we saw her?"

"I'm sure we would."

"I wonder what she's doing right now."

The boys added their flowers one at a time. Patrick continued to hold his. We read some of the nearby markers. I was amazed at how many babies had died recently. My heart went out to the parents, whose grief would still be fresh. I wondered about *their* stories.

The boys began to get restless. One by one, they headed back to the van. Patrick and I remained on the grass, united in our silence. He spoke. "Seven years. It doesn't seem possible."

"I know. It's hard to believe."

More silence. Patrick took his daisy and slowly brushed its petals down my face. He sat up and pulled me toward him and tenderly kissed me.

"I love you," he said softly.

"I love you, too." I could barely speak.

He eased himself up and crouched near the head of the marker. With great care, he placed his daisy stem in the middle of the others and arranged the delicate flowers. As I watched him lovingly merge his flower into ours and carefully tend to it, I suddenly became aware of tears wetting my cheeks. Once again I marveled at my tears. They were so unexpected, yet so refreshing. It was good to remember.

Patrick stood and reached out for me. He put his arm around me as we walked toward the van with our closeness wrapped around us like a child's favorite quilt. I whispered through my tears, "I'll *always* miss her."

He gently squeezed my shoulder and quietly replied, "I know."

# RECOMMENDED READING

## OTHER BOOKS ON PREGNANCY LOSS

*After a Loss in Pregnancy: Help for Families Affected by a Miscarriage, a Stillbirth or the Loss of a Newborn* by Nancy Berezin. Simon and Schuster, 1982.

*Coping with a Miscarriage* by Hank Pizer and Christine O'Brien Palinski. Dial Press, 1980.

*Surviving Pregnancy Loss* by Rochelle Friedman, M.D., and Bonnie Gradstein, M.P.H. Little, Brown and Co., 1982.

*When Pregnancy Fails: Families Coping with Miscarriage, Stillbirth, and Infant Death* by Susan Borg and Judith Lasker. Beacon Press, 1981.

These books all describe the emotional and physical response to pregnancy loss experienced by the mother, father, and other family members. They provide solid medical information and discuss options for the future.

---

*Empty Arms: Emotional Support for Those Who Have Suffered Miscarriage or Stillbirth* by Pam W. Vredevelt. Multnomah Press, 1984.

*Free to Grieve: Healing and Encouragement for Those Who Have Experienced the Physical, Mental, and Emotional Trauma of Miscarriage and Stillbirth* by Maureen Rank. Bethany House Publishers, 1985.

Each of these books was written by a Christian woman who experienced pregnancy loss. They stress the necessity of grieving, but also hold out the hope that grieving will end.

---

*Misty, Our Momentary Child* by Carole Gift Page. Crossway Books, 1987.

A mother shares the pages of her journal written before, during, and after the short life of Misty, her "momentary" child. Christ was at the center of this woman's journey through sorrow to healing.

---

*Nothing to Cry About* by Barbara J. Berg. Seaview Books, 1981.

One woman's story of pregnancy losses, adoption, and successful pregnancy.

---

*Swimmer in the Secret Sea* by William Kotzwinkle. Avon, 1975. (Also in *Redbook Magazine,* July 1974).

A novella written from the father's perspective on the stillbirth of his son.

---

*Taste of Tears, Touch of God* by Ann Kiemel Anderson. Oliver-Nelson Books, 1984.

Ann candidly shares her pain and sorrow as she experienced pregnancy losses waiting for a baby that wasn't to be. In the process she came to accept sorrow as her friend and to wait for God's time.

## MATERIALS ON PREGNANCY LOSS
## FROM MEDICAL CENTERS

### Oregon Health Sciences University:

*When Hello Means Goodbye: A Guide for Parents Whose Child Dies at Birth or Shortly After* by Pat Schwiebert, R.N., and Paul Kirk, M.D., 1981.

This 32-page pamphlet is full of practical advice on coping with the loss of a child at birth.

---

*Still to Be Born: A Guide for Bereaved Parents Who Are Making Decisions about Their Future* by Pat Schwiebert, R.N., and Paul Kirk, M.D., 1986.

This 112-page book begins where *When Hello Means Goodbye* ends. It blends poetry and writings from bereaved parents with practical information for parents who are grieving the loss of a child and wanting another child but are afraid of being hurt again by another loss.

---

These two publications are available from: Perinatal Loss, 2116 N.E. 18th Avenue, Portland, OR 97212. Or call (503) 284–7426.

**Resolve through Sharing, La Crosse, Wisconsin:**

This group has published a beautifully illustrated *Parents' Booklet* which sensitively helps couples deal with pregnancy loss. They also have shorter brochures on subjects such as *Miscarriage, Ectopic Pregnancy, Grandparents' Grief,* and *Autopsy.*

---

These materials are available from: Resolve through Sharing, La Crosse Lutheran Hospital/Gunderson Clinic Ltd., 1910 South Avenue, La Crosse, WI 54601.

## BOOKS ON GRIEF AND LOSS

*A Gift of Hope: How We Survive Our Tragedies* by Robert L. Veninga. Ballantine Books, 1985.

A couple mourning the loss of a stillborn child is one of the many examples in this book of moving from grief to hope.

---

*Creative Suffering* by Paul Tournier. Harper and Row, 1982. This book has a particularly good chapter on anger.

---

*Life Is Goodbye — Life Is Hello: Grieving Well through All Kinds of Loss* by Alla Bozarth-Campbell. Comp-Care Publications, 1982.

*Living through Personal Crisis* by Ann Kaiser Stearns. Ballantine Books, 1984.

*Turn to Life Again: Growing through Grief* by Abraham Schmitt. Herald Press, 1987.

Facing grief seems like the unnatural response to loss. These three authors believe that grieving our losses leads to healing and freedom.

## BOOKS ON JOURNAL WRITING

*How to Keep a Spiritual Journal* by Ronald Klug. Thomas Nelson, 1982.

Klug believes that a spiritual journal can give you the time and structure to explore your life—to learn about your feelings, thoughts, dreams, relationships to others and God, gifts, and beliefs.

*Letters to Scattered Pilgrims* by Elizabeth O'Connor. Harper and Row, 1979.

This book includes two chapters on journal keeping along with a wealth of material on personal and spiritual growth.

---

*The New Diary: How to Use a Journal for Self-Guidance and Expanded Creativity* by Tristine Rainer. J. P. Tarcher, 1979.

This book advocates journal keeping as a way of knowing oneself better. Several different methods of journal writing are exposed.

## BOOKS ON THE SPIRITUAL LIFE

*Disappointment with God: Three Questions No One Asks Aloud* by Philip Yancey. Zondervan, 1988.

Yancey tackles the crises of faith caused by a God who doesn't always do what we think he should. Yancey searches for the answers to three questions—Is God unfair? Is God silent? Is God hidden?

*Space for God: The Study and Practice of Prayer and Spirituality* by Don Postema. Bible Way, 1983.

This book encourages us to make space for God in our lives and includes a good chapter on "Wrestling with God."

*When You're Angry at God* by Father William Rabior. Liguori Publications, 1984.

A short pamphlet that reveals the healthy side of religious anger.

*Where Is God When It Hurts?* by Philip Yancey. Zondervan, 1977.

Yancey gives personal glimpses into the lives of people who have experienced crisis, pain, and suffering. He grapples with the difficulty of relating one's personal faith to experiences of loss and pain.